DATE DUE

D1116856

Religions
of the World

Catholicism

Don Nardo

LUCENT BOOKS
An imprint of Thomson Gale, a part of The Thomson Corporation

THOMSON
™
GALE

Detroit • New York • San Francisco • San Diego • New Haven, Conn. • Waterville, Maine • London • Munich

*The author dedicates this volume with love
and respect to Paul and Diane.*

© 2006 by Lucent Books. Lucent Books is an imprint of The Gale Group, Inc.,
a division of Thomson Learning, Inc.

Lucent Books® and Thomson Learning™ are trademarks used herein under license.

For more information, contact
Lucent Books
27500 Drake Rd.
Farmington Hills, MI 48331-3535
Or you can visit our Internet site at http://www.gale.com

LIBRARY OF CONGRESS CATALOGING-IN-PUBLICATION DATA

Nardo, Don, 1947–
  Catholicism / by Don Nardo.
    p. cm. — (Religions of the world)
  Includes bibliographical references and index.
    ISBN 1-59018-632-X (hard cover : alk. paper) 1. Catholic Church—
History—Juvenile literature. I. Title. II. Series: Religions of the world
(San Diego, Calif.)
  BX948.N37 2005
  282—dc22
                                                                2005019737

Printed in the United States of America

Contents

Foreword

Religion has always been a central component of human culture, though its form and practice have changed through time. Ancient people lived in a world they could not explain or comprehend. Their world consisted of an environment controlled by vague and mysterious powers attributed to a wide array of gods. Artifacts dating to a time before recorded history suggest that the religion of the distant past reflected this world, consisting mainly of rituals devised to influence events under the control of these gods.

The steady advancement of human societies brought about changes in religion as in all other things. Through time, religion came to be seen as a system of beliefs and practices that gave meaning to—or allowed acceptance of—anything that transcended the natural or the known. And, the belief in many gods ultimately was replaced in many cultures by the belief in a Supreme Being.

As in the distant past, however, religion still provides answers to timeless questions: How, why, and by whom was the universe created? What is the ultimate meaning of human life? Why is life inevitably followed by death? Does the human soul continue to exist after death, and if so, in what form? Why is there pain and suffering in the world, and why is there evil?

In addition, all the major world religions provide their followers with a concrete and clearly stated ethical code. They offer a set of moral instructions, defining virtue and evil and what is required to achieve goodness. One of these universal moral codes is compassion toward others above all else. Thus, Judaism, Christianity, Islam, Hinduism, Buddhism, Confucianism, and Taoism each teach a version of the so-called golden rule, or in the words of Jesus Christ, "As ye would that men should do to you, do ye also to them likewise" (Luke 6:31). For example, Confucius instructed his disciples to "never impose on others what you would not choose for yourself" (*Analects:* 12:2). The Hindu epic poem,

Mahabharata, identifies the core of all Hindu teaching as not doing unto others what you do not wish done to yourself. Similarly Muhammad declared that no Muslim could be a true believer unless he desires for his brother no less than that which he desires for himself.

It is ironic, then, that although compassionate concern for others forms the heart of all the major religions' moral teachings, religion has also been at the root of countless conflicts throughout history. It has been suggested that much of the appeal that religions hold for humankind lies in their unswerving faith in the truth of their particular vision. Throughout history, most religions have shared a profound confidence that their interpretation of life, God, and the universe is the right one, thus giving their followers a sense of certainty in an uncertain and often fragile existence. Given the assurance displayed by most religions regarding the fundamental correctness of their teachings and practices, it is perhaps not surprising that religious intolerance has fueled disputes and even full-scale wars between peoples and nations time and time again, from the Crusades of medieval times to the current bloodshed in Northern Ireland and the Middle East.

Today, as violent religious conflicts trouble many parts of our world, it has become more important than ever to learn about the similarities as well as the differences between faiths. One of the most effective ways to accomplish this is by examining the beliefs, customs, and values of various religions. In the Religions of the World series, students will find a clear description of the core creeds, rituals, ethical teachings, and sacred texts of the world's major religions. In-depth explorations of how these faiths changed over time, how they have influenced the social customs, laws, and education of the countries in which they are practiced, and the particular challenges each one faces in coming years are also featured.

Extensive quotations from primary source materials, especially the core scriptures of each faith, and a generous number of secondary source quotations from the works of respected modern scholars are included in each volume in the series. It is hoped that by gaining insight into the faiths of other peoples and nations, students will not only gain a deeper appreciation and respect for different religious beliefs and practices, but will also gain new perspectives on and understanding of their own religious traditions.

Modern Challenges for an Ancient Faith

Today, there are about a billion Catholics in the world, making up nearly one-sixth of the planet's total population. They make up the largest single denomination of Christianity, which boasts an overall membership of some 2 billion adherents. The heaviest concentrations of Catholics are in North and South America and Europe, but numbers of converts to the faith are steadily growing in Africa and Asia. No matter where they live, all Catholics recognize the leadership of the Church's chief bishop— the pope. He resides in the Vatican, a tiny nation-state situated within the city limits of Rome, Italy.

Although Catholicism, overseen by the pope and other bishops, is today one of many denominations in the larger Christian tent, this was not always the case. In fact, from Christianity's beginnings in Roman-controlled Palestine in the first century A.D. to the advent of the Reformation in the 1500s, the Christian Church and Catholic Church were the same entity. Only when Martin Luther and other rebel clergymen challenged the authority of the popes during the Reformation did other Christian denominations spring into being and begin competing with Catholicism. But although bruised by the Reformation, the Catholic Church survived the great schism and remains strong and widely influential.

A Global Impact

Indeed, both before and after the Reformation, the Church has consistently been one of the fundamental pillars of Western (European-based) society. It rose from obscurity and weathered numerous Roman persecutions to become Rome's official religion. Subsequently, following Rome's fall in the fifth and sixth centuries, the Church became the spiritual guide for most of Europe. Church doctrine (beliefs, rules, and policies) colored the thinking, customs, and habits of people of all walks of life, often on the most basic levels. Over the course of the Middle Ages and beyond, hundreds of thousands of people went even further and devoted their lives to the Church by becoming priests, monks, and nuns. Because many of them lived in monasteries, religious retreats separate from the rest of society, this became known as the monastic movement.

Pope Benedict XVI greets a group of nuns after a mass celebrated in Rome in June 2005. The pope is the Church's spiritual leader.

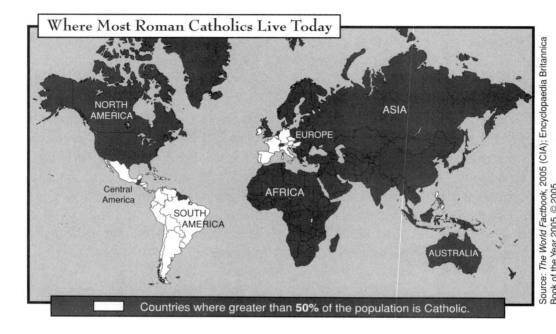

Where Most Roman Catholics Live Today

NORTH AMERICA

EUROPE

ASIA

Central America

AFRICA

SOUTH AMERICA

AUSTRALIA

Countries where greater than **50%** of the population is Catholic.

Source: *The World Factbook*, 2005 (CIA); Encyclopaedia Britannica Book of the Year 2005. © 2005.

The impact of the Church on the postmedieval world was equally great. In the late medieval and early modern eras, missionaries brought the Church's ideas and morals and often political authority to the Americas and other parts of the world. At the same time, following the Reformation, Protestant groups took their message to these same foreign shores. These Christians, with their increasingly diverse views, no longer identified themselves with the Catholic Church. Yet it has been argued that, in the larger historical sense, the newer Christian denominations represented, and today still represent, part of the overall impact of Roman Catholicism on world history. After all, just as Judaism (the religion of the Jews) gave birth to and made possible Christianity, Catholicism gave birth to and made possible all other Christian groups and ideas.

The Catholic Church has proven to be long-lived and in numerous ways highly influential. It has also been, with occasional exceptions, extremely well organized and disciplined, with a clear-cut chain of command stretching downward from the pope in Rome to local parishes across the globe. These have been the major factors in the Church's success as a world religion. Indeed, whether one agrees with Catholic doctrine or not, no one can deny that the Church has been phenomenally successful. As the noted modern Catholic theologian Hans Kung puts it:

> Beyond question the history of the Catholic Church is a history of success. The Catholic Church is the oldest, numerically the strongest, and probably also the most powerful representative of Christianity. There is a great admiration [among members of all faiths] for the vitality of this two-thousand-year-old church; for its organization, which was global before any talk of global-ization, and at the same time effective locally. . . ; for its worship, rich in tradition and colorful in its splendor; [and] for its indisputable cultural achievements in building up and shaping the West.[1]

Diversity and Disagreement in the Ranks

Although venerable, large, powerful, and successful, the modern Catholic Church is not by any means monolithic. That is, not all Catholics have the same opinions on political, social,

The fact that not all Catholics think alike is illustrated by disagreements on various issues. Here, priests in New York march in support of gay Catholics.

or even religious issues. In fact, except on the Church's core writings, beliefs, and practices—such as the scriptures, the divinity of Jesus Christ, and the sacraments (baptism, Communion, and so forth)—Catholic groups and communities across the world differ widely on most issues. "Though it has a very centralized government in the Vatican, in Rome," Oxford University scholar Keith Ward points out, the Church

> is in practice very diverse. There are very traditional Catholics, who wish to see a . . . politically conservative church . . . [guided mainly by] the Pope. There are very radical Catholics, who ally themselves with those who fight for liberation from . . . political and economic oppression. . . . There are Catholics who oppose the alleged . . . humanism of the secular [nonreligious] world . . . and there are Catholics who embrace the European Enlightenment as liberating faith from outmoded forms of thought. So while it is possible to say what the official attitude of the Vatican is, it is much more difficult to make any accurate generalizations about what Catholics throughout the world actually believe.[2]

As a result of this diversity of thought within the ranks of its membership, there is considerable disagreement about how the Church should deal with the many challenges it faces in the modern world. Among these challenges are several involving priests. There is an increasing shortage of recruits for the priesthood, for instance. And a number of Catholics, especially in the United States, have called for allowing priests to marry and for women to be allowed to be ordained in the priesthood. Financial woes that have led to a number of

With an open prayer book, a Catholic priest waits for word of the election of a new pope in April 2005.

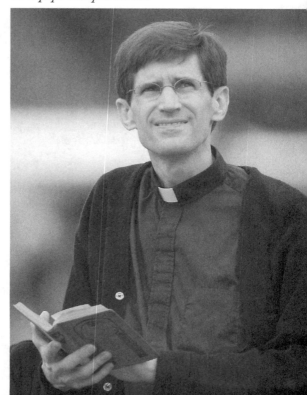

church closings are also high on the agenda of challenges that Church officials must deal with. Some of these financial problems stem from lawsuits brought against priests accused of molesting children, and the sexual misconduct of priests is itself a matter of great concern to Church leaders.

Still another challenge, say some prominent Catholics, is for the Church to try harder to maintain its traditional obligation to aid the poor. "At a time when the global gap between rich and poor widens every year," journalist and former priest James Carroll writes, "will the Catholic Church survive as one of the few institutions that inherently bridges the gap?" The Church "has also been a force for progressive social change," Carroll adds. "Will it continue to be?"[3] The answers that Catholics, both clergy and laypersons, end up providing for this and other crucial questions will decide the future path of an ancient faith that is ever struggling to retain relevance and authority in a rapidly changing modern world.

chapter | one

The Church's Ancient Origins and Birth

It is not by accident that the oldest surviving Christian denomination still has its main headquarters in Rome and calls itself the Roman Catholic Church. Nor is it by mere chance that today's Catholics, as well as members of other Christian denominations that sprang from Catholicism, retain numerous beliefs, rituals, and customs that developed in ancient Roman society. This is because Catholicism, which was one and the same with Christianity at that time, was born and nurtured in the early Roman Empire. In the mid– to late first century A.D., when that birth occurred, the Romans controlled the entire Mediterranean world. Their realm stretched from Spain in the west to Palestine in the east, and from North Africa in the south to southern Britain in the north.

The Romans provided the early Church with two very useful tools that proved crucial in its development. First, the sprawling Roman realm had an extensive system of excellent roads and was then largely at peace and very prosperous, factors that made it easier for the Christians to spread their beliefs. As noted historian of Christianity Justo Gonzalez puts it:

The political unity wrought by the Roman Empire allowed the early Christians to travel without having to fear bandits or local wars. . . . Well-paved and well-guarded roads ran to the most distant provinces. Since trade flourished, travel was constant. Thus, Christianity often reached a new region, not through the work of missionaries or preachers, but rather

A carved scene on a third-century coffin unearthed in Rome shows a Christian man baptizing a young boy.

through traveling traders, slaves and others.[4]

The other useful tool Rome provided the early Church was a rich cultural melting pot from which to draw religious ideas, practices, and customs. In the first century A.D., the Roman Empire was made up of many different peoples with diverse ethnic, intellectual, and religious backgrounds. The early Christians were strongly influenced by many of the ideas in this Mediterranean melting pot. But they were particularly influenced by the beliefs and customs of the Jews, since the Christian movement was at first an offshoot of Judaism.

Jewish Struggles and the Messiah

Indeed, the Church's Jewish roots are revealed by a number of uniquely Jewish ideas and customs that the Christians kept even after they had broken away from Judaism. First, Catholics (and other Christians) view their single, all-powerful God as one and the same with the Hebrew God of the Old Testament. Second, the monotheistic Jews had always seen themselves as set apart from other people, both spiritually and culturally, and Christianity inherited this feeling of special exclusivity. The two faiths also share the same ethical tradition, which emphasizes the stability of family

Early Influences on Christianity

Early Christianity had many elements in common with the other Eastern faiths— sometimes called mystery religions—that spread through the Roman realm shortly before or after the dawn of the Empire. This was partly because most of these faiths borrowed ideas from one another, whether consciously or unconsciously. Scholar Charles Freeman explains in Egypt, Greece, and Rome.

Much of the imagery of the New Testament—light and darkness, faith compared to flourishing crops—is similar to that found in mystery religions. The "facts" of Jesus's life were presented in a format which was not unique to him. . . . The promise of an afterlife for the initiated would have been commonplace to anyone who had contact with mystery religions. The development of the cult of Mary, the mother of Jesus, acquires a new richness when placed in parallel with the worship of other mother figures in these religions.

life, chastity, and helping the poor and sick. Probably most important of all, the Catholic Church inherited from the Jews the scriptures, which Christians came to call the Old Testament. These books, beginning with Genesis, describe the creation of the world by God, Noah's flood, the deeds and teachings of Moses and other prophets, and the struggles of the ancient Jewish kingdoms of Israel and Judah.

It is possible that these ideas and writings would have forever remained exclusively Jewish had it not been for a succession of Jewish struggles for survival. For many centuries, the Jews' most holy city, Jerusalem, and the rest of Palestine had been repeatedly overrun by foreign armies. Babylonians, Persians, Greeks, and others had conquered the Jews and left their marks on the region.

But no people left a bigger mark than the Romans, who first intervened in the area in the mid–first century B.C. Rome did not impose direct rule on Palestine right away, however, and at first was content to install local Jewish leaders as puppet rulers. But soon the Romans changed their minds. In A.D. 6 they turned much of Palestine into the Roman province of Judaea and assigned a Roman governor to take charge.

These turbulent events inspired much disagreement and rivalry among the Jews. Each of a number of political and religious factions in the Jewish community had its own views about how to deal with the Romans, as well as how to interpret God's laws. Yet all of these factions agreed on certain fundamental points. For instance, they all revered the scriptures. Also, they all believed that the Messiah, "the anointed one," a superhuman or divine figure, would come to Earth to rescue the Jews from their centuries-long oppression. It was widely thought that the Messiah would bring about the kingdom of God, a utopian age of divine rule and eternal salvation. A first-century-B.C., Jewish text described the supposed imminent arrival of the Messiah this way:

This shall be a time of salvation for the people of God, an age of dominion for all the members of His company, and of everlasting destruction for all the company of Satan. . . . The [enemies of the faithful, including the Romans] shall come to an end and iniquity shall be vanquished, leaving no remnant. . . . And at the season appointed by God, His exalted greatness shall shine eternally to the peace, blessing, glory, joy, and long life of all the sons of light. . . . Rise up, O Hero! Lead off Thy captives, O Glorious One![5]

Catholicism's Bedrock: Jesus

Those Jews who eventually separated themselves from Judaism and became Christians believed that the Jewish preacher Jesus of Nazareth was this Messiah of prophecy. At the time, other Jewish sects disagreed. In their view, Jesus was simply one of numerous holy men who preached strict adherence to God's laws and advocated that God's kingdom was imminent. John the Baptist, the traveling preacher who baptized Jesus, was another.

In fact, this disagreement over whether or not Jesus was the Messiah

In this engraving, Judas kisses Jesus to identify him to the soldiers who have come to arrest him. Soon afterward, Jesus was crucified.

A First-Century Description of Jesus

Only a few ancient non-Christian literary references to Jesus have survived. One of the more substantial ones appears in the Jewish historian Josephus's Jewish Antiquities, *dating from the year 93, about sixty years after Jesus's death. (The bracketed phrases were added later by Christian scribes to make it seem as though Josephus accepted Jesus's divinity, which in fact the historian did not.)*

About this time there lived Jesus, a wise man, [if indeed one ought to call him a man]. For he was one who wrought surprising feats and was a teacher of such people as accept the truth gladly. He won over many Jews and many of the Greeks. [He was the Messiah.] When Pilate, upon hearing him accused by men of the highest standing among us, had condemned him to be crucified, those who had in the first place come to love him did not give up their affection for him. [On the third day he appeared to them restored to life, for the prophets of God had prophesied these and countless other marvelous things about him.] And the tribe of the Christians, so called after him, has still to this day not disappeared.

was one of the major reasons that the Christians broke away from Judaism. The Catholic Church eventually came to see the life and teachings of Jesus Christ as its basic bedrock. (His given name was Jesus; the name Christ came from the Greek word *Christos*, meaning "Messiah," and was used by his followers only after his death.)

Most of what little is known about Jesus's life comes from the four Gospels—Matthew, Mark, Luke, and John—which eventually became the first four books of the New Testament. These writings tell about Jesus's birth in the small Palestinian town of Bethlehem. They also describe his preaching among the Jews, how he gained his first close followers (the twelve apostles, or disciples), and how he was said to have performed various miracles. In addition, the Gospels recount how Jesus ran afoul of Jewish and Roman authorities in Jerusalem and how he was arrested and executed by crucifixion. It appears that Jesus died in about A.D. 30 at roughly the age of thirty-three or thirty-four.

The People of "the Way"

Religious scholars agree that Jesus himself did not set out to establish a new faith. Nor did his apostles and other early followers intend to do so. The key events of the birth of the Catholic Church occurred in the years immediately following Jesus's death. First, according to the Gospels, he rose from the dead. When some of his followers went to visit his tomb soon after his execution, they found the stone chamber empty. Then, the story goes, Jesus appeared to several of his followers and told them, among other things, "It is written, that the Christ should suffer and on the third day rise from the dead, and that repentance and forgiveness of sins should be preached in his name to all nations, beginning from Jerusalem."[6]

After these supernatural happenings, Jesus's closest followers started telling people that he had been the Messiah. And because the Messiah had recently walked the earth, God's kingdom must truly be at hand. At the time, in fact, these followers of Jesus, who initially called themselves the "People of the Way," thought he would return and establish that glorious kingdom at any moment, certainly in their own lifetimes.

At first, the People of the Way still thought of themselves as Jews. "This is why Christians in Jerusalem continued keeping the Sabbath [the Lord's holy day] and attending worship at the [Jewish] Temple," Gonzalez points out. "To this they added the observance of the first day of the week, in which they gathered in celebration of the resurrection of Jesus."[7] Not surprisingly, therefore, the People of the Way initially aimed their message about Jesus's divinity and the imminent coming of God's kingdom solely at other Jews.

But most Jews did not accept that the prophecy of the Messiah had been fulfilled. They grew suspicious of the People of the Way, seeing them as possible heretics (people who reject the traditional religious beliefs and rules), and began persecuting them. Two of the group's leaders, the apostles Peter and John, were arrested, beaten, and ordered to stop preaching. They and most of their fellow believers showed their defiance and determination by setting up new chapters outside of Jerusalem, in the Syrian cities of Damascus and Antioch. Yet no matter where they went, they continued to find it hard to find new converts. Many historians think that, had they continued to preach only to Jews, the Catholic Church and other Christian denominations may never have come to be.

Paul Makes the Church Possible

It was at this point, in about the year 36, that the key figure in the foundation of the Church entered the picture. He was Saul of Tarsus, later called Paul, a Jew who had become a Roman citizen. He had been one of the many people who had persecuted the People of the Way. But then, on the road to Damascus, he later explained, he had a vision of the resurrected Jesus. "You have heard of my former life in Judaism," Paul later said,

> how I persecuted the Church of God violently and tried to destroy it.... But when he who . . . had called me through his grace [i.e., God] was pleased to reveal his Son [Jesus] to me, in order that I might preach [about] him among the gentiles [non-Jews], I did not confer with flesh and blood [but rather, he spoke with the Holy Spirit].[8]

This speech emphasized what Paul viewed as the primary mission God had given him—to bring word of Jesus's divinity to the gentiles. This idea was not completely new. In fact, some of the People of the Way had already considered trying to convert non-Jews. However, they knew that this would be very difficult, mainly because most gentiles

This Renaissance painting captures the moment when Saul of Tarsus, later St. Paul, had a divine vision.

were reluctant to join a Jewish organization. In part, this stemmed from the Jews' image as a stubborn, exclusivist people who refused to accept the existence of other people's gods. Even more important, most gentiles did not like the idea of having to adopt certain Jewish customs, especially circumcision and strict dietary laws.

Paul had the brilliant realization that dropping these requirements for gentiles might attract many new converts who would swell the ranks of the People of the Way. And he persuaded the group's elders in Jerusalem to adopt this course in about 49. In the years that followed, he and other early believers traveled across the Roman world, utilizing its huge network of roads as well as merchant ships that stopped at numerous distant ports. In preaching to people far and wide, they consistently "established that a gentile could become a Christian without previously going over to Judaism," Hans Kung writes.

> With this program and [their] restless . . . missionary work [Paul and his associates] had a resounding success with the mission to the gentiles. . . . Only in this way could a little Jewish sect become a world religion. . . . To this extent, it is no exaggeration to say that there

would have been no Catholic Church without Paul.[9]

Early Church Organization

The more that non-Jews joined the followers of Jesus, the more inevitable it became that the group would, sooner or later, cease to be Jewish. By the 50s A.D. its gentile members who lived outside Jerusalem had come to call themselves Christians. A majority of the Jewish Christians still dwelled in Jerusalem. But most of them died during a failed Jewish rebellion against Rome in the 60s. Meanwhile, in other sectors of the Mediterranean world, gentile Christians soon came to greatly outnumber Jewish Christians. This trend continued, and by the late first century nearly all Christians viewed themselves as separate from the Jewish faith and culture.

By the early second century, therefore, at least several dozen small non-Jewish Christian communities existed in various parts of the Roman Empire. News and correspondence moved slowly—by foot, horse, or ship. So, many of the outlying communities were often out of touch with the larger and more influential communities, such as those at Antioch and Rome. This created the potential for some Christian enclaves to

When Was Jesus Born?

The consensus of present scholarship is that Jesus was born about 4 B.C., the year that the Roman-supported Jewish ruler King Herod died. At first glance this may sound strange, since "B.C." means "before Christ" and the calendar presently used across the Western world supposedly started counting years from Jesus Christ's birth. It is therefore only natural to ask why Jesus was not born in A.D. 1. The answer is that the calendar in question was not created and put into place until the sixth century, by which time the exact dates of many events of the early Roman Empire were uncertain. The Christian monk who invented the calendar (Dionysius Exiguus) made educated guesses about these dates, including that for the death of Herod. Modern studies have shown, however, that these guesses were off by at least four years.

develop their own ideas and organization and break away from the greater Church community. To prevent this from happening, Church leaders sought to standardize the Church's organization and practices and to impart these standards to Christians everywhere.

A leader in this endeavor was Ignatius of Antioch (ca. 35–107). He was the first known Christian to refer to the Church as "catholic," meaning universal or everywhere united under the same beliefs. In letters to various Christian communities, he insisted that unity could be fostered by denying membership to anyone who did not accept Jesus's divinity. Ignatius also advocated the creation

of a hierarchy (ladder) of authority within the Church. Each Christian, or Catholic, community came to have one strong overall leader—the bishop (from the Greek word *episkopos*, meaning "overseer"). And each bishop was assisted by elders, called presbyters and deacons, who performed a wide range of clerical and other duties. "Follow your bishop," Ignatius urged, "as Jesus Christ followed the Father; and [follow] the presbyters as the apostles; and to the deacons pay respect, as to God's commandment."[10]

The Persecutions

During these formative years in which the infant Catholic Church struggled to gain new converts and achieve an effective, standardized organization, it also had to fight for its very existence. This is because some non-Christian, or pagan, Romans harassed, attacked, and at times even arrested and killed Christians. These persecutions were generally sporadic, with periods of relative quiet and safety between large-scale, violent epi-

The early Christian leader Ignatius of Antioch was the first to refer to the Church as "catholic."

sodes. Also, it was common for the authorities to persecute Christians in one region while leaving Christians in other areas alone.

The reasons for these persecutions are frequently misunderstood today. The Romans did not institute them because they were intolerant of other peoples' beliefs. In fact, the Romans were among the most religiously tolerant people in history and had no problem with the Christians worshipping their own god. Indeed, in the Roman religious melting pot, which included numerous and diverse faiths and gods, members of one faith routinely showed respect for the gods of other faiths.

The Christians insisted that their God was the only god, however, and therefore that all other gods must be false. Most non-Christians were deeply offended by what they viewed as a lack of respect for others' beliefs, and came to see Christians as atheists because of their refusal to accept the existence of all gods. Many pagans feared that a hard core of atheists in their midst might bring down the wrath of the gods on the Empire. Also, based on misconceptions about the Church's rituals, many pagans thought that incest, cannibalism, and baby killing were regular features of Christian worship. Finally, the Chris-

The Apologists

During the persecutions, a few Christian leaders took on the task of explaining and defending Christian beliefs to make the faith more acceptable to pagans. Because their written defenses of the faith were called apologies, they became known as apologists. One influential apologist was Tertullian (ca. 160–240). Far from being a threat to society, Tertullian said, the Christians were good Romans who were loyal to both Rome and the emperor. In his Apology *(quoted in Lewis and Reinhold's* Sourcebook 2*), he stated:*

"You [Christians] do not," say you, "worship the gods; you do not offer sacrifice for the emperors." . . . So that is why Christians are public enemies—because they will not give the emperors vain, false, and rash honors; because, being men of a true religion, they celebrate the emperors' festivals more in heart than in frolic. . . . For we invoke the eternal God, the true God, the living God for the safety of the emperors. . . . Looking up to heaven, the Christians—with hands outspread, because [they are] innocent . . . are ever praying for all the emperors. We pray for a fortunate life for them, a secure rule, a safe house, brave armies, a faithful senate, a virtuous people, a peaceful world.

tians refused to recognize the divinity of Rome's emperors, which the government interpreted as a potential threat to its authority and to public order.

For these reasons, the members of the early Catholic Church came to be seen as subversive and possibly even dangerous. The conventional reasoning was that they should be watched and when necessary punished to ensure that they did not hurt "ordinary" people. With tremendous tenacity and courage, the Christian community weathered nearly three centuries of periodic persecution, all the while waiting and hoping for a Roman leader with the guts, vision, and heart to reach out to them and their God. He finally appeared in the early fourth century, and his name was Constantine.

chapter two

The Spiritual Guide for Medieval Europe

The legends, poetry, books, and movies of Western civilization are filled with colorful images of the Catholic Church in the medieval era, or Middle Ages. (Historians usually date this period from the fall of Rome, in the late fifth century, to about 1600.) Among these often quaint but also powerful images are monks and nuns praying in secluded monasteries in the countryside; armies of knights with crosses painted on their banners as they march off to fight enemies of the faith; and the majestic spires of Gothic cathedrals pointing skyward as if reaching toward God.

These and other historical snapshots evoke what was indeed a unique and pivotal era. For more than a thousand years, the Church, its beliefs and practices, and its clergy profoundly affected nearly every aspect of life in the kingdoms that succeeded the Roman Empire in Europe. (These realms were founded by the so-called barbarians who had overrun Rome and later grew into the nation-states of Europe.) Catholicism became the unchallenged spiritual guide for medieval Europe, as well as a potent shaper of political and social norms and customs. The Church also inspired and guided the actions of many of the European explorers who reached the Americas and other formerly unknown lands. As a result, the Church spread overseas.

None of this could or would have happened if the long-persecuted Christians had not risen to take control of the Roman government and put themselves in a position to inherit the wreckage of Rome after it fell. Once it got started, that rise was extremely rapid. And it was made possible in large part by the foresight and policies of one remarkable man—the emperor Constantine I (reigned 307–337). He granted the Christians toleration and economic privileges; he erected the first Christian city, Constantinople; and he eventually converted to the faith.

These and other deeds and policies Constantine and his successors initiated allowed the Church to triumph as Rome's official religion. It was transformed from the Catholic Church into the Roman Catholic Church, with the wealth of benefits that came with the name *Roman*. "To the future of Christianity its official adoption by the Empire

A monk gives a cross to a soldier, who will carry it into battle. During the Middle Ages, many battles were fought in the name of God and the Church.

Constantine's Miraculous Vision

The Christian bishop Eusebius wrote a biography of the emperor Constantine (quoted here from volume 1 of Brian Tierney's The Middle Ages). *On the day before the battle at the Milvian Bridge, Eusebius claimed, Constantine had a divinely inspired vision. Most modern historians think that Eusebius fabricated the event later, to make the emperor look more holy, or that Constantine misinterpreted some natural phenomenon.*

[At] about noon, when the day was already beginning to decline, he saw with his own eyes the trophy of a cross of light in the heavens, above the sun, and an inscription, CONQUER BY THIS, attached to it. At this sight he himself was struck with amazement. . . . And while he continued to ponder and reason on its meaning, night overtook him; then in his sleep the Christ of God appeared to him . . . and commanded him to make a likeness of that sign which he had seen in the heavens, and to use it as a safeguard in all engagements with his enemies.

was momentous," the late, great classical scholar A.H.M. Jones pointed out. In this way, the Church

acquired the prestige and glamour of the Roman name. It became synonymous with that ancient civilization whose grandiose buildings, stately ceremonial, luxurious life, and discipline fascinated the uncouth barbarians of [northern Europe]. Inevitably [both before and after Rome's fall] they copied Roman ways, and with the rest of Roman culture adopted the Roman religion.[11]

Constantine Becomes the Church's Benefactor

The rise of Roman Catholic Europe began in earnest in 312. At the time, Constantine was one of several ambitious men who claimed the throne of the Roman Empire. In the climax of a series of civil conflicts, he marched his army into Italy with the goal of unseating one of his rivals, Maxentius, who had taken control of Rome. The opposing armies clashed at the city's Milvian Bridge. Constantine was victorious and gained complete control of the western half of the Empire.

In retrospect, the most important aspect of the battle was that the winners believed they had been aided by the Christian God. Years before, when Constantine and his father had been in charge of the province of Gaul, they had refused to harass the Church and its members during the last of the government's anti-Christian persecutions (launched in 303). Some kind of trust or friendship seems to have subsequently developed between Constantine and the Church, and his soldiers painted a Christian symbol on their shields just prior to the battle at the Milvian Bridge.

Thankful for the help he had received from the Christians, Constantine thereafter showed them increasing support and favoritism. A major milestone occurred in 313 when he (together with the emperor who was then ruling the Empire's eastern sector) issued the so-called Edict of Milan. It granted official toleration to Christians throughout the Empire, saying in part: "We resolved to issue decrees by which . . . all Christians [will have] freedom of choice to follow the ritual which they wish."[12] In the years that followed, Constantine's support for the Christians remained strong. He erected churches for them all over the realm. And he mediated several serious disputes that arose among the bishops, whom he recognized as the faith's political, as well as spiritual, leaders.

The Roman emperor Constantine demonstrated strong support for Christians.

Another boost the Church received from Constantine was his establishment of Constantinople, "the city of Constantine," on the Bosporus Strait on the Black Sea's southern rim, in May 330. His main goal was to create a line of defense against attacks from the east. But from the beginning, the new city was also conceived as a Christian stronghold. In its inaugural ceremony, in fact, the emperor dedicated it to the Virgin Mary.

Constantine further increased the Church's prestige and potential for gaining both new converts and political power when he himself formally converted to the faith. This momentous event—including his baptism—occurred in 337 when he was on his deathbed. By this time he was a committed Christian and wanted to set an example for his successors, as well as for ordinary Romans.

Rome's Official Religion

The example that Constantine set, coupled with his other pro-Church policies, proved to be a great turning point, not only for Christianity but also for Rome and European civilization in general. Following his passing, the Church enjoyed rapid and spectacular growth. Constantine's sons were all devout Christians,

as were all but one of the emperors who succeeded them. In their religious zeal, these leaders confirmed and extended the privileges their father had given the Church's bishops and priests, including exempting them from paying taxes and making them immune from prosecution by secular courts.

As more and more high-ranking Romans joined the Church, its leaders and practices came under the influence of the Roman imperial court and its wealthy trappings. One result was that the ceremonies attending Christian worship became more formal and splendid. Priests adopted the burning of incense, for example, which had long been done at court as a sign of respect for the emperor. Also, people were now expected to bow to the bishops just as they did to the emperors and members of the royal family. In addition, the bishops began dressing in more elaborate and luxurious garments styled after the formal wear of Roman noblemen.

At the same time, the Church grew progressively larger, richer, and more politically powerful, partly at the expense of Roman pagans and their own time-honored institutions. Membership in the Church swelled. Some of the converts joined because they were attracted by

Christian beliefs, especially the promise of salvation after death. But others, seeing the Christian takeover of the government, reasoned that converting would bring them social or political advantages. Some of the new converts were wealthy and donated money and land to the Church. Others aided the clergy in attacking paganism. In the last decades of the fourth century, militant Christians smashed pagan statues and vandalized or even destroyed pagan temples all across the Empire, while zealous Christian priests denounced pagan beliefs from the pulpit. In a stunning reversal, Christian scholar Tony Lane writes, "the persecuted church of the martyrs" became "the persecuting state church."[13]

These efforts to stamp out non-Christian ideas and worship were spearheaded by a brilliant but self-righteous bishop named Ambrose of Milan (born ca. 340). Thanks to his influence, the emperors gave up the post of *pontifex maximus*, chief priest of the traditional state religion. Ambrose also convinced the

A Renaissance artist painted this likeness of Ambrose, the bishop who convinced a series of Roman emperors to grant the Church benefits and power.

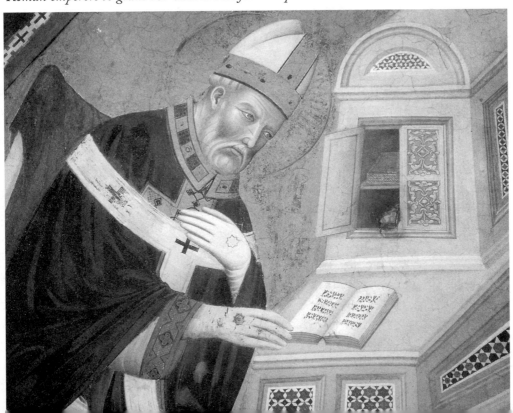

government to confiscate the funds of the state priesthood and to remove the time-honored statue of the goddess Victory from Rome's Senate House. Finally, in the 390s Ambrose got the emperor Theodosius I to abolish all pagan sacrifices and cults and officially close all pagan temples. After Ambrose's death in 397, his role as chief spokesman for the Church fell increasingly on the bishops of Rome. They came to be called popes (from a word meaning "father") and in the fifth century emerged as the overall leaders of the Church.

In astonishingly little time, therefore, the Catholic Church managed to achieve a controlling influence over Rome's leaders and major institutions. But this was not the full extent of the Church's influence. It also extended downward into all levels and facets of society, including local parishes and even the simple worship that average people performed in their homes. So when western Rome's government fell to the barbarian tribes of central and northern Europe in the fifth century, the Church's social apparatus survived.

Catholicism Spreads Across Europe

This turn of events seemed to fulfill a prediction made by Augustine and other influential Roman Christian thinkers during western Rome's final century of existence. Rome was mortal, they had said. And like other earthly cities before it, sooner or later it would pass away. But the Church, with its direct ties to God, was eternal and would therefore survive.

In fact, many people in Italy and other parts of Europe now looked to the popes and other members of the clergy to provide the sort of guidance, order, and stability that had traditionally come from government leaders and institutions. "It was the Church that provided continuity with the past," Justo Gonzalez explains. "She became the guardian of civilization and of order. In many ways, she filled the power vacuum left by the demise of the Empire."[14]

In the century immediately following that demise, the popes exercised their power partly by sending out missionaries to convert those barbarians who had not already accepted Christian beliefs. In this way, more and more of western Europe became Christianized. The great Frankish king Clovis, whose kingdom spanned much of the former Roman province of Gaul, converted to Catholicism in 496. And many other barbarian rulers swiftly followed suit.

The populations of the British Isles remained largely pagan a good deal longer, however. The conversion of pagan England was under-

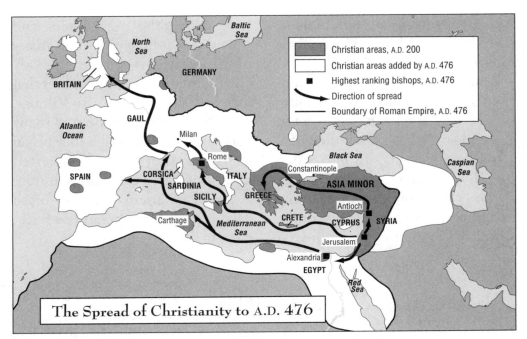

The Spread of Christianity to A.D. 476

taken in earnest by Pope Gregory I (born ca. 540). In 596 or 597, he sent a group of about forty young monks to England. They established a cathedral and a school at Canterbury (east of London), which later became the center of the Church of England.

During this process of converting western European pagans to Catholicism, one of the Church's most potent and effective tools was the monastic movement. It was based on the idea of achieving a closer relationship with God by accepting a life of extreme self-discipline and self-denial. Daily life for the inhabitants of a monastery consisted of manual labor, supplemented by pray-

ers and other devotions. Often, as they worked in the fields or made clothes or prepared meals, they prayed, sang hymns, and/or recited passages from the Bible. They also helped the poor in their respective regions and spread Catholic beliefs to other regions.

Many monasteries were established, and thousands of people became monks in Rome's last two centuries. The movement continued to expand in the early medieval centuries. Particularly influential was the Benedictine order, founded in Italy in the sixth century. This group recorded its rules and routines in a written document that became known as the *Rule*. It soon became a sort of blueprint for hundreds of monasteries established across Europe in the following centuries.

Though these peaceful approaches to conversion were often quite successful, some people resorted to force to spread the Catholic faith. On Christmas Day in 800, Pope Leo III crowned Charlemagne, king of the Franks, emperor of what the two hoped would be a new Roman Empire. Charlemagne conquered several neighboring peoples and forced Catholic baptism on many of those who were not already Christians. In the two centuries that followed, the Norsemen, or Vikings, from Scandinavia, terrorized many parts of Europe. Though they began as pagans, they quickly converted and joined the Catholic Church. And like Charlemagne, they often used coercion to spread the faith, even to other Vikings.

Charlemagne's Pact with the Pope

In 795 the Frankish king Charlemagne wrote a letter to the newly ordained pope, Leo III. In this excerpt quoted in Weber's The Western Tradition, *Charlemagne expresses his eagerness to spread Catholicism far and wide, including by the use of force.*

I want to establish with [you] an inviolable [unbreakable] pact of faith and charity by which . . . the very holy seat of the Roman Church can be constantly defended. . . . It is my part to defend everywhere the Holy Church of Christ by armed force, on the one hand against pagan raids and devastation of the unbelievers; on the other hand by the diffusion [spread] of Catholic faith. It is your part, most holy father . . . to help by your prayers the victory of our arms.

The emperor Charlemagne (seated at left) receives an oath of homage from one of his barons.

The Offensive Against Islam

These and other zealous efforts to spread Catholicism were highly successful in Europe, but the Church encountered trouble when it tried to establish a European power base in the Near East. European Christians had long made pilgrimages to Palestine—the so-called Holy Land—to visit biblical sites. Though Muslims controlled Palestine, the local authorities had usually not interfered with the religious pilgrims. But in the mid–eleventh century the warlike Seljuk Turks, who had recently converted to Islam, took over most of the Near East, including Palestine.

Back in Rome, Church leaders wanted to see European Catholics drive the Turks out of Jerusalem and seize direct control of the Holy Land. So in 1095 Pope Urban II called for the formation of a great military expedition. Over the course of the next two centuries, at least seven such expeditions, which came to be known as the Crusades, were launched. The crusaders enjoyed some successes at first. The soldiers of the First Crusade captured Jerusalem in July 1099, for instance.

But this and other early victories were possible only because the Muslims were not yet well organized in the region. Also, the cru-saders often betrayed their lofty religious goals by using unnecessarily brutal means. When they took Jerusalem in 1099, for example, as Gonzalez puts it:

> There followed a horrible blood-bath. All the defenders were killed, as well as many civilians. Women were raped and infants thrown against walls. Many of the city's Jews had taken refuge in the synagogue, and the crusaders set fire to the building with them inside.[15]

Not surprisingly, these tactics back-fired. Many of the later Crusades were less successful, and the last two were complete disasters that ended with the Muslims once again in charge of Palestine. Mistrust and hatred between Christians and Mus-lims lingered for many centuries.

Catholicism Spreads to New Lands

It was not long after the Church's offensive against Islam failed that a new avenue for the spread of Catholic beliefs and power materialized. In the late 1400s Christopher Columbus, an Italian explorer sailing for Spain, made landfall in the Americas. In the years that followed, Spanish and Portuguese explorers and settlers

The Road to Jerusalem: The Routes and Events of the First Crusade

Pope Urban II addresses the Church council and calls for the First Crusade in 1095.

In 1099 crusaders attack the city of Jerusalem.

ENGLAND

GERMANY

Bruges

Bouillon

Regensburg

Vezelay

North Atlantic Ocean

HUNGARY

FRANCE

Clermont

Venice

Zara

BULGARIA

Black Sea

Toulouse

Pisa

Durazzo

Constantinople
Bosporus

Marseille

ITALY

SPAIN

Rome

Bari

Nicaea

Naples

Dorylaeum

Brindisi

SICILY

Edessa
Antioch

Tripoli

Mediterranean Sea

CYPRUS

Tyre

CRETE

Acre

Jerusalem

N
W   E
S

Routes of the First Crusade

established colonies on the coasts and islands of North, Central, and South America. Similar colonies were later established in Africa, the Pacific Islands, and Asia. The explorers, settlers, and their sponsors back in Europe were all devout Catholics and saw it as their duty to convert the "heathen" (non-Christian) natives to their faith.

In the long run, this enterprise was phenomenally successful, as millions of people joined the Church in the course of only two centuries. But as

The Leading Catholic Thinker

The leading Catholic thinker of the Middle Ages was Thomas Aquinas. In his great masterwork the Summa Theologica (Sum of Theology) *and other writings, he sought to explain the mysteries of nature and religion using reason and logic. In this example from the* Summa Theologica, *he applies logic to the question of whether God exists.*

The existence of God can be proved . . . from the [way the world is governed]. For we see that things that lack intelligence, such as natural bodies, act for some purpose. . . . It is plain that not fortuitously [by chance], but designedly [by design], do they achieve their purpose. Whatever lacks intelligence cannot fulfill some purpose unless it is directed by some being endowed with intelligence and knowledge. . . . Therefore, some intelligent being exists by whom all natural things are ordained towards a definite purpose; and this being we call God.

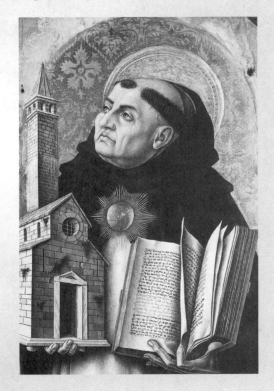

Thomas Aquinas attempted to use logic and reason to prove the existence of God.

in the case of the Crusades, the methods employed exacted a tremendous cost in human misery. Native Americans and other original inhabitants of the conquered and colonized lands were systematically exploited and abused. Many became indentured servants—not much better off than slaves—to settlers entrusted with teaching them Catholic beliefs and practices.

Nevertheless, some Catholic missionaries—notably monks in the Dominican, Jesuit, and Franciscan monastic orders—recognized the natives' plight and tried to help them. One of the more prominent of these men was a Dominican named Bartolomé de Las Casas. He spent more than four decades trying to persuade Spanish authorities to treat the natives more humanely. He also wrote a number of controversial books that called into question the morality of European colonial and religious policies in the Americas. Unfortunately, the Church eventually banned his books. And the exploitation of the natives continued, although many of those who were well treated by the monks converted to Catholicism willingly.

Ironically, even as the Church was gaining large numbers of new members, it was losing many traditional ones. During the very same years that Las Casas and other missionaries argued with Church authorities, those authorities were unable to stop millions of Europeans from joining new, non-Catholic Christian groups. It was the greatest challenge the Church had faced since the Roman persecutions more than a thousand years before. And the chance was very real that this time it would not survive.

chapter three

Major Threats: The Reformation and Modernism

The 1500s marked a momentous turning point for European and world civilization. In that century the medieval era rapidly drew to a close, partly because of new scientific advances and also because European explorers were opening up vast new territories in distant parts of the globe. Just as important a factor in this grand transition of Western civilization was the Reformation, in which the Catholic Church, long Europe's single, monolithic faith, was torn asunder. So-called Protestant groups broke away from Roman Catholicism. And by the end of the sixteenth century, Europe was divided into a mix of Catholic and Protestant countries.

This extreme outcome was not what the Protestant reformers had originally intended. They believed that the Church had become corrupt. They charged that its leaders and practices had strayed too far from the basic Christian principles on which the faith had been founded and called for reform. Yet as the late and respected scholar G.R. Elton pointed out, these reformers initially "did not want to found [new] churches. They wanted to reform the one and only Church. . . . They

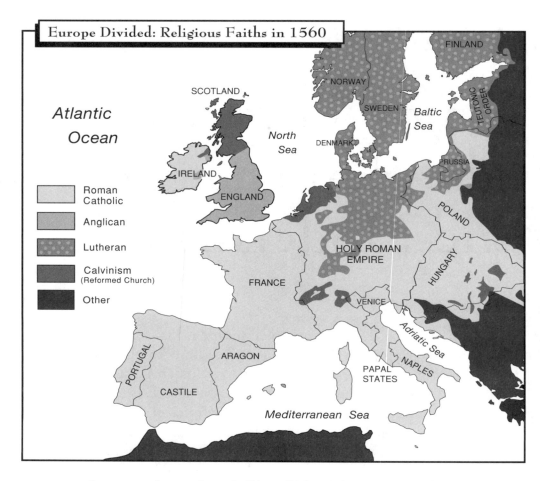

Europe Divided: Religious Faiths in 1560

Atlantic Ocean

SCOTLAND

IRELAND

ENGLAND

North Sea

DENMARK

NORWAY

SWEDEN

FINLAND

Baltic Sea

TEUTONIC ORDER

PRUSSIA

POLAND

HOLY ROMAN EMPIRE

FRANCE

HUNGARY

VENICE

Adriatic Sea

PORTUGAL

ARAGON

CASTILE

PAPAL STATES

NAPLES

Mediterranean Sea

Roman Catholic
Anglican
Lutheran
Calvinism (Reformed Church)
Other

meant to cleanse and transform it."[16] However, most high-ranking Church leaders stubbornly resisted change, and the result was a permanent schism that ended up producing many new Christian denominations.

With great difficulty, the Catholic Church weathered this huge blow to its organization and prestige. This was partly because Church leaders eventually recognized that some reform was necessary; without it, the faith might not survive. But even while the Church's recovery was under way, it found itself facing other threats, some of them no less formidable than those posed by the Reformation. Among these new challenges was the rise of modern science, which is concerned with logic and evidence rather than faith. Also, the same brand of rational thought that motivated the scientists spilled over into politics. Political reformers began demanding human rights and democracy, and democratic thinkers and reformers increasingly promoted the idea of secular government, in which church and state would be kept separate. Over time, these and other onrushing forces of modernism significantly reduced the once towering authority and influence of the Catholic Church in European society.

Corruption and Demands for Reform

None of these challenges affected the power and reputation of the Church more than the Reformation, however. Historians usually date its start to 1517. This was the year that German monk and theology professor Martin Luther (1483–1546) publicly issued a list of charges

Luther Criticizes the Pope and Church

In 1520, shortly after the pope excommunicated Martin Luther, the latter wrote his Address to the German Nobility, *excerpted in Bernard and Hodges's* Readings in European History, *in which he summarized some of the basic religious and political principles of the ongoing Reformation.*

Martin Luther called on the Church to institute numerous reforms, but to no avail.

The Pope should have no power over the Emperor, except to anoint and crown him at the altar, as a bishop crowns a king. . . . The custom of kissing the Pope's feet must cease. It is an un-Christian, or rather an anti-Christian example that a poor sinful man should suffer his feet to be kissed by one who is a hundred times better than he. . . . We see also how the priesthood is fallen, and how many a poor priest is encumbered with a woman and children and burdened in his conscience. . . . My advice is to restore liberty, and to leave every man free to marry or not to marry. . . . It is one of the most urgent necessities to abolish all begging. . . . No one should go about begging among Christians.

against the Church. At the time, he was upset that priests and popes were selling indulgences (partial pardons for confessed sins) for a profit and thereby taking advantage of the faithful. But soon he and other reformers, including Swiss priest Ulrich Zwingli (1484–1531) and French theologian John Calvin (1509–1564), took the Church to task for many other abuses. One modern survey of Catholicism summarizes their grievances:

> [The Church's] hierarchy was corrupt and disorganized. Wealthy families staffed the leadership positions of churches. . . . These members of the clergy bought and sold clerical positions. Bishops controlled huge territories . . . that increased their own revenues, and Church officials bought and sold indulgences. Meanwhile, the local clergy was not properly educated and did not make much effort to take care of their flocks. . . . They set a bad example. Some had drinking problems, and others kept mistresses. Religious orders were no better off. . . . Discipline in monasteries had waned, and members were no longer concerned about social and cultural conditions in the countryside.[17]

Luther addressed all of these problems and more in a series of critical writings that rocked the Church and European society. He condemned the selling of indulgences, saying: "Christians should be taught that he who sees anyone in need, and, passing by him, gives money for pardons, is not purchasing for himself the indulgences of the Pope but the anger of God." And he added: "Vain is the hope of salvation through letters of pardon, even if . . . the Pope himself were to pledge his own soul for them."[18] Luther also criticized the excess wealth and luxury enjoyed by the pope, the bishops, and the bloated bureaucracy of unnecessary officials he said surrounded them. The pope "must abolish the papal offices," Luther thundered,

> and diminish that crowd of crawling vermin at Rome, so that the Pope's servants may be supported out of the Pope's own pocket, and that his court may cease to surpass all royal courts in its pomp and extravagance.[19]

Such open and stinging attacks on the Church and its leaders did not endear Luther to the reigning pope, Leo X. Luther received a number of warnings to cease his critiques, but he ignored them. As a result, in 1520

Leo excommunicated Luther (expelled him from the Church). This act only made the brash reformer more popular with his fast-growing army of supporters, who were ready to follow him in breaking free of the Church and founding a new branch of Christianity. Indeed, by the mid-1520s, Lutheranism was well established in many parts of Europe.

Meanwhile, John Calvin sent missionaries to Scotland, the Netherlands, and other parts of Europe, where millions of people eventually converted to his brand of Protestantism (which became known as the Reformed Church). In the same century, England's King Henry VIII and his daughter, Elizabeth I, launched their own offensive against Catholicism. The result was the formation of another Protestant denomination—the Anglican Church. By 1546, the year Luther died, fully half the population of Europe had turned its back on the Catholic Church and embraced rival Christian faiths.

The Church Reacts to the Reformation

This was truly the Church's lowest ebb, and many Europeans viewed it as a dying institution. But Catholicism was like a tough, courageous boxer who refuses to stay down and allow himself to be counted out. When things appeared darkest for the Church, it made a concerted effort to reform and to some extent reinvent itself. These efforts were successful and in less than a generation the Church sprang back, recouped some of its losses, and kept Protestantism from making a clean sweep of Europe. Collectively, these efforts later became known as both

England's King Henry VIII separated his country from the Catholic Church, forming the Anglican Church.

the Counter-Reformation and the Catholic Reformation.

One of the earliest and most crucial elements in this reform movement was an honest attempt at self-analysis and self-criticism. Realizing the Church was in serious trouble, in 1537 Pope Paul III appointed a commission of high-ranking clergy to investigate corruption and abuses within the organization. (The investigation and its report were intended to remain secret but soon leaked out and became public.) The commissioners did find widespread abuses and diligently reported them to the pope. Typical among their findings were the following:

> In the ordination of [priests], no diligence is employed. The most ignorant men . . . and adolescents are admitted to . . . the priesthood. . . . A great abuse that should be reformed is the granting of payments to rich clerics, who can live quite comfortably . . . on the revenues they already have. . . . [Bishops] should not absent themselves from their churches and parishes . . . [yet] almost all pastors have left their flocks [and involved themselves in worldly affairs].[20]

The pope and other reformers decided that these and other systemic problems must be addressed and if

possible corrected. Also, the Church's outward image and prestige needed to be refurbished. Hoping to accomplish both of these goals, in 1540 Church leaders gave their approval to a new monastic order—the Society of Jesus, or Jesuit order—which had been established by Ignatius Loyola six years before. The Jesuits dedicated themselves to strict vows of poverty, obedience, honesty, and charity. "Let

This etching adorned the cover of a Jesuit writing. The Jesuits took strict vows of poverty and obedience.

us with the utmost pains," one vow went,

> strain every nerve of our strength to exhibit this virtue of obedience, firstly to the [pope], then to the superiors of society [kings, nobles, and the like]; so that in all things . . . we may be most ready to obey his voice, just as if it issued from Christ, our Lord.[21]

The hope was that, as they went out into communities across the globe, the Jesuits would set an example of how the Church was returning to its spiritual roots. This plan worked. Through their diligence and good works, the Jesuits helped to revive confidence in the Church and in so doing slowed the growth of Protestantism.

Another important element of the reform effort was the Council of Trent, which consisted of three major meetings of Church leaders held between 1545 and 1563. The goals were to better define what true Catholicism was so that the Church could get back to its roots and to impose better discipline at all levels of Church organization. The council reminded Catholics that salvation could not be bought, but rather, could come only through charity and other good works. Bishops and other clergy were required to stay with their flocks and to reside near their churches; the granting of indulgences was regulated; and priests were required to receive basic educations in seminaries and to remain celibate. The Council of Trent proved the definitive statement of Catholicism in response to the Protestant Reformation and to a great extent shaped the Church's practices and image for more than three centuries.

The Onset of the Enlightenment

The Counter-Reformation, coupled with the influx of new converts from overseas, ensured new centuries of life for the Church. But there was little rest for its defenders and policy makers. They had no sooner dealt with the Church's internal problems when they were besieged by a host of external ones. These challenges questioned the authority of the popes and the Church as a whole, and made a number of Catholics question their own faith.

The most sweeping of the challenges was the onset of the European Enlightenment in the 1600s. The Enlightenment was an intellectual movement conceived mainly by liberal English and French thinkers. It was driven by its appeal to and celebration of human reason, newly discovered scientific facts, religious toleration, the existence of certain basic natural human rights, and fair government. Enlightenment philosophers held that science might reveal the true nature of the world, which humans could then in essence remake, controlling and exploiting it to their advantage. Part of this rebirth, they suggested, was a new understanding of human nature, emphasizing certain inherent rights, including freedom of thought, the right of self-expression, and individual personal fulfillment.

Throughout the 1600s and 1700s, the Enlightenment's liberal theories slowly but steadily and profoundly transformed the way that educated people in Europe and America viewed certain political and social institutions that had been taken for granted for many centuries. Among these institutions were the Catholic Church and formal, traditional religions in general. The Church now had to compete with and try to remain relevant in the face of the principal underlying concept of the Enlightenment—reason, which was driven by cold logic and factual evidence. Indeed, there was a fear among the Church's guardians that the champions of reason might try to sweep away religion and replace it with their seemingly godless philosophy. "Human reason is modernity's leading value," Hans Kung points out.

Reason now increasingly becomes the arbiter [judge] of all questions of truth. Only the rational is regarded as true, useful, and binding. Philosophy is given precedence over theology; nature . . . over grace, the human over the specifically Christian. . . . [In the 1600s] belief in the omnipotence of reason and the possibility of dominating nature developed. It became the foundation for the modern idea of progress. . . . Progress was assigned almost divine attributes. . . . Human self-determination and human power over the world—a substitute religion for more and more people—had been born.[22]

Initial Reactions to Reason and Science

The Enlightenment, which at first worried and distressed Church leaders, did not materialize out of nowhere. It was inspired by the rise of science in Europe. Particularly influential were the work and ideas of Polish astronomer Nicolaus Copernicus (1473–1543), who showed that the Sun, rather than Earth, lies at the center of the solar system (known as the heliocentric theory), and Frenchman René Descartes (1596–1650), sometimes called the "father" of modern mathematics.

A Philosopher Pokes Fun at Kings and Popes

In 1721 the French philosopher Voltaire, one of the leading figures in the European Enlightenment, published his Persian Letters. *They contain satires of the major institutions of his age, especially the French monarchy and Catholic Church. In this excerpt, translated in Bernard and Hodges's* Readings in European History, *he criticizes the king and pope for abusing their great powers.*

The king is a great magician, for his dominion extends to the minds of his subjects. He makes them think what he wishes. . . . If he has a costly war on hand, and is short of money, he simply suggests to his subjects that a piece of [worthless] paper [money] is [equivalent to gold] coin of the realm and they are straightaway convinced of it. . . . What I have told you of this prince need not astonish you. There is another magician more powerful still, who is master of the king's mind, as absolutely as the king is master of the minds of his subjects. This magician is called the Pope. Sometimes he makes the king believe that three are no more than one [a reference to the Trinity, consisting of Father, Son, and Holy Spirit]; [and] that the bread which he eats is not bread [a reference to Communion, in which Catholics eat bread symbolizing Christ's body].

The French philosopher Voltaire was known for his biting critiques of long-established institutions, including the Church.

These and other scholars provided a firm foundation for the philosophical ideas of Enlightenment thinkers such as England's John Locke (1632–1704), France's Voltaire (1694–1778), and America's Thomas Jefferson (1743–1826).

This fundamental connection between science and Enlightenment ideas was not lost on the leaders of the struggling Catholic Church. They recognized that a number of scientific discoveries conflicted with some long-cherished beliefs based on biblical passages. Copernicus's vision of Earth revolving around the sun, for example, seemed to contradict the phrase "The Lord . . . has made the world firm, not to be moved."[23] This passage had always been interpreted to mean that Earth did not and could not move. If Copernicus was right, the Bible must be wrong and therefore not infallible, as had been widely accepted. Church leaders saw this and other new scientific discoveries as threats to the established religious and social order.

Thus, initially the Church viewed the rise of science and the onset of the Enlightenment with a great deal of fear and anxiety. And this explains why its leaders at first overacted in negative and sometimes hurtful ways. Copernicus's and Descartes's books were banned, for instance. Some philosophers, as well as priests, who accepted their views, were burned at the stake. And when the Italian scientist Galileo (1564–1642) used a new invention, the telescope, to show that Copernicus was right, the Church tried him for heresy and placed him under house arrest. In the long run, however, these attempts to stop the march of science failed. And the harsh manner in which the Church initially dealt with the challenge posed by science proved counterproductive and hurt the image of Catholicism.

The Specters of Democracy and Secularism

A similar scenario played out when the Church began to face one of the most potent and far-reaching outgrowths of the Enlightenment—the rise and spread of liberal democracy and the secular ideas associated with it. For more than a thousand years the Church had had a working relationship with emperors, kings, princes, and other absolute rulers. (In fact, to a considerable degree, the hierarchy of the Church itself had been patterned after monarchies and their royal courts.) Church leaders were used to having working relationships with secular leaders and directly influencing their actions and policies. So, the notion of separating religion and politics and leaving the Church out of the corridors of power disturbed and worried Church leaders.

This was especially true of the French Revolution, which began in 1789. It directly affected the Church because many of the French were still devout Catholics. When the revolutionaries reduced the Church's political power and tried to secularize the institution in France, Pope Pius VI called the Revolution invalid. He also roundly denounced the principles of human rights, equality of all human beings, and freedom of religion. Like the earlier conservative reaction to science, this hard-line stance against the unstoppable wave of modern democracy backfired. "The chief victim" of the Revolution "was the Catholic Church," Kung writes. It lost not only its power over national leaders but also

Polish astronomer Nicolaus Copernicus proposed that the Earth revolves around the Sun, an idea the Church at first resisted.

its secular power, which extended to education, hospitals, and care to the poor, and also its tremendous property [in land and other valuables]. Instead of a culture governed by the Church and clergy, a secularized, republican culture emerged.[24]

The results were similar as new democracies rose in various parts of the globe in the years that followed. Clearly, Church leaders felt that they had to find a way to make up for their losses in power, property, and prestige. The question was whether or not this was possible in an increasingly modernized world.

chapter four

The Church's Stalwart Anchor: The Pope

Throughout most of its history, the Catholic Church's most familiar symbol (besides the crucifix) has been its spiritual and political leader, the pope. Once it became well established in the fifth century, the papacy became the top rung in the Church's ladder of authority, and the popes had the final say in making and enforcing the organization's rules and policy. Moreover, in the Middle Ages and beyond, the popes wielded enormous influence over secular leaders and the everyday lives of faithful Catholics in Europe and eventually across the world.

Like the Church itself, the papacy originated in Italy, more specifically in the city of Rome. Rome was, and remains, the seat of power for nearly all

The dome of St. Peter's Basilica, located in Vatican City, was designed by Renaissance artist and architect Michelangelo.

of the popes, and that partially explains why the vast majority of popes have been of Italian birth. Of the more than 260 popes who have presided over the Church, 205 of them have been Italian. Of the others, 19 were French; 14 were Greek; 8 were Syrian; 5 were German; 3 were African; 2 were Spanish; 1 was Austrian; 1 was Palestinian; 1 was English; 1 was Dutch; and 1 (the recently deceased John Paul II) was Polish.

Some of these many popes are remembered better than others. Several, including Leo I, Gregory I, Gregory VII, and John XXIII, came to be seen as strong leaders who set important precedents and/or advanced the Church's causes and position. Many earned reputations for deep spirituality and good works, and of these, eighty-one were declared saints following their deaths. In contrast, other popes came to be seen as weak or counterproductive, even evil.

However good or bad or effective or ineffective past popes may have been, today Catholics around the world continue to revere the papal office. The prevailing belief is that, despite the fact that human beings choose the pope, God has some kind of indirect hand in the process. Thus, many Catholics see the pope as a true intermediary between the faithful and the divine, as well as a spiritual guide and anchor for thousands of parishes scattered across the globe.

Origins of the Papacy

In fact, the metaphor of the pope as a strong, stalwart anchor for the Church is far from new. According to tradition, the first Christian parish in Rome—the precursor of the central institution of the Catholic Church—had been established by Peter, one of Jesus's most trusted disciples. "I tell you," Jesus is said to have told Peter, "on this rock [meaning Peter himself] I will build my church, and . . . I will give you the keys of the kingdom of heaven."[25] Because the evidence is sparse, modern scholars are unsure whether Peter actually founded the first Christian community in Rome. It is also unclear whether at this point there was a single bishop in charge of that community or a council of leaders.

However, most ancient and medieval Church leaders accepted the above passage, from the Gospel of Matthew, at face value. In fact, a prominent bishop of Rome, Leo I (reigned 440–461), routinely quoted this passage to justify two major claims. First, Leo asserted, Jesus's comments indicated that he wanted Peter to be the leader of all his followers (those who would later become known as Christians); and second, the bishops of Rome were Peter's direct successors and therefore deserved to be, like Peter himself, the overall leaders of the Church. "The blessed Peter," Leo declared,

> has not abandoned the helm of the church which he undertook. . . . [He] may be recognized and honored in [the form of] my humble person . . . and his dignity is not lessened even in so unworthy an heir. . . . When therefore [I give you orders], holy brethren, believe that he [Peter] is speaking whose representative [I] am.[26]

Although the bishops of other Roman cities often argued with Leo on this point, he acquired a great deal of authority and preeminence in other ways. In 452 the Huns, a barbarian group from Asia, invaded Italy. Leo bravely went out and met with the Hunnish leader, Attila, and somehow convinced him not to sack the city of Rome. About three years later, another barbarian group, the Vandals, did enter Rome and looted it. Once more, Leo arranged for a meeting with the intruders' leader and in this

case persuaded him to refrain from burning the city. As a result of these and other notable acts, Leo eventually came to be widely seen as the leader of the entire Church, and later generations viewed him as the first true pope.

Even more influential in defining the papacy and solidifying its authority was Gregory I (born ca. 540), who became Rome's bishop about three generations after western Rome's fall. In addition to sending monks to convert the pagans in England, he set numerous standards that later medieval and modern popes would follow. At the time, Italy had been invaded by still another barbarian group—the Lombards—and the city of Rome was suffering from food shortages and a disease epidemic. Rome also lacked an effective secular leader. So Gregory took charge. He kept Rome safe from the Lombards and ruled the city and its surrounding region for a period of several years, deeds that established the pope as a political as well as spiritual leader. He then used what he had learned in the secular sphere to reorganize the Church into an elaborate and smoothly running bureaucracy. Gregory also wrote the *Pastoral Rule*, which became the standard manual of conduct for medieval bishops.

Pope Gregory I ruled the city of Rome effectively and set down rules and standards for the bishops to follow.

Papal Authority Ebbs and Flows

Partly because the papacy had developed into a wealthy, powerful institution, it, like all such institutions in history, became increasingly open to corruption by greedy, self-serving individuals. In the eighth century, the papacy began to decay. In Justo Gonzalez's words, it became "easy prey" for ambitious, deceitful, violent men:

Pope succeeded pope in rapid sequence . . . as the papacy became the prize for which the various rival parties in Rome and beyond . . . fought. Popes were strangled, or died of starvation in the dungeons where they had been thrown by their successors. At times there were two popes or even three, each claiming to be the one true successor to Saint Peter.[27]

Eventually, some strong, honest popes appeared and initiated major reforms. Prominent among them was Leo IX (reigned 1048–1054), who overhauled the clergy and increased the authority and prestige of high Church officials called cardinals (from the Italian word *cardines*, meaning "hinges"). Another important reformer, Pope Gregory VII, reaffirmed the authority of the

51

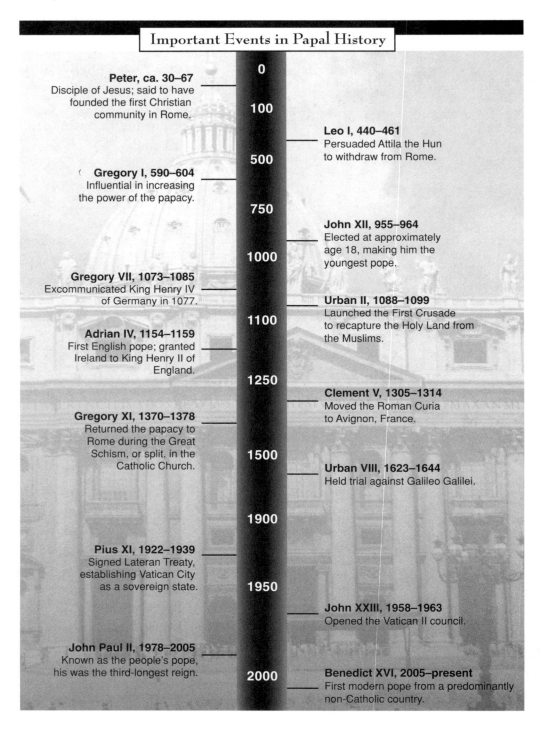

Important Events in Papal History

Peter, ca. 30–67
Disciple of Jesus; said to have founded the first Christian community in Rome.

Leo I, 440–461
Persuaded Attila the Hun to withdraw from Rome.

Gregory I, 590–604
Influential in increasing the power of the papacy.

John XII, 955–964
Elected at approximately age 18, making him the youngest pope.

Gregory VII, 1073–1085
Excommunicated King Henry IV of Germany in 1077.

Urban II, 1088–1099
Launched the First Crusade to recapture the Holy Land from the Muslims.

Adrian IV, 1154–1159
First English pope; granted Ireland to King Henry II of England.

Clement V, 1305–1314
Moved the Roman Curia to Avignon, France.

Gregory XI, 1370–1378
Returned the papacy to Rome during the Great Schism, or split, in the Catholic Church.

Urban VIII, 1623–1644
Held trial against Galileo Galilei.

Pius XI, 1922–1939
Signed Lateran Treaty, establishing Vatican City as a sovereign state.

John XXIII, 1958–1963
Opened the Vatican II council.

John Paul II, 1978–2005
Known as the people's pope, his was the third-longest reign.

Benedict XVI, 2005–present
First modern pope from a predominantly non-Catholic country.

0
100
500
750
1000
1100
1250
1500
1900
1950
2000

papacy, in effect depicting the pope as a universal ruler who stood above secular kings as well as all Church officials. He demonstrated this authority in dramatic fashion in 1077. When Gregory forbade the historic practice by which European kings chose their own local bishops, Germany's King Henry IV refused to obey. The pope then stunned all of Europe by excommunicating Henry. In an astonishing display, the greatest monarch on the Continent was forced to stand barefoot in the snow for days until Gregory forgave and reinstated him.

Though Gregory and others carried the papacy to a high point in its history, in time it once again grew corrupt. Indeed, papal authority and prestige continued to ebb and flow for centuries. Yet most of the popes maintained a certain minimal level of power because they were the rulers of

Gregory Expands Papal Power

In the late eleventh century, Pope Gregory VII defined the expanding scope of papal authority in a decree known as the Dictatus Papae *(quoted in J.H. Robinson's* Readings on European History*).*

The Roman Church was founded by God alone. The Roman bishop alone is properly called universal. He alone may depose bishops and reinstate them. . . . He alone may use the insignia of empire. The Pope is the only person whose feet are kissed by all princes. His title is unique in the world. He may depose emperors. No council may be regarded as a general one without his consent. . . . He may be judged by no one. . . . The Roman Church has never erred, nor ever, by the witness of Scripture, shall err to all eternity. He may not be considered Catholic who does not agree with the Roman Church.

Pope Gregory VII redefined and expanded papal authority.

Vatican City

Switzerland

Austria

ITALY

Slovenia

Croatia

Bosnia

EUROPE

ASIA

AFRICA

Corsica

Rome

Sardinia

Tyrrhenian
Sea

Sicily

AFRICA

Vatican City, a sovereign state within Rome,
is ruled by the pope and serves as the
headquarters of the Roman Catholic Church.

a country as well as leaders of the Church. In the 750s, the reigning pope had helped Pepin the Short gain the French throne. And King Pepin had shown his gratitude by giving the Church a parcel of land spanning large parts of northern and central Italy. This became the basis for the so-called Papal States, which emerged as an independent nation by the year 1300. Though control of the Papal States was sometimes contested, its territory continued to expand and reached its greatest extent in the 1700s.

The popes' power as secular rulers, however, was not destined to continue. In 1798 the French, led by Napoléon Bonaparte, invaded Italy, and the reigning pope, Pius VI, had to flee into exile. After Napoléon's decline, the Papal States was briefly restored to the papacy. In 1860, however, Italian nationalists declared Italy a sovereign nation and drastically reduced the size of the Papal States. Ten years later, an Italian army attacked the Papal States, which promptly ceased to exist. Finally, in February 1929 the Church signed a treaty with the Italian government to create a new nation for the popes to rule. Called Vatican City, it became the world's tiniest country, encompassing less than 109 acres inside Rome's city limits.

The Pope and His Church Hierarchy Today

Today, the pope remains the absolute monarch and ruler of Vatican City. However, the modern popes do not have the time to deal with the day-to-day duties of running a country. So each pope appoints some cardinals to actually run Vatican City. One cardinal acts as the president, another as secretary of state, and so forth.

Meanwhile, the pope concentrates his time and energies on running the Catholic Church itself. Once chosen to fill the papal office, the pope serves for life and has the last word in all of the Church's legal and spiritual policies and decisions. Following historical precedent, the pope is viewed as the highest-ranking bishop in the hierarchy of Catholicism.

Other rankings of bishops exist directly below the pope in that hierarchy, which is structured largely like a pyramid. The cardinals, who make up an organization called the College of Cardinals, are the highest-ranking bishops in the Church other than the pope. They both choose the popes (from among their own number) and advise them. The cardinals also run the pope's administrative arm within the Church—the Roman Curia. The Curia is divided into departments, or offices, like the government of a typical country. These departments include the sectretariat of state, which coordinates all the others, and offices that deal with Church law; administration of the dioceses (geographic territories in which Catholics live); missionary work; and numerous other matters.

Below the pope and cardinals in the Vatican, the pyramid of the Church's hierarchy widens into the dioceses, which span the globe. Each diocese is governed by a bishop or archbishop (the highest ranking bishop below the cardinals). A popular Catholic handbook lists the major duties of a bishop this way:

> He can adopt laws for his diocese that the faithful must follow. . . . He acts as judge in any [religious] matter. . . . He is expected to reside within his diocese for most of the year and to be present at his cathedral church during [major Church observances, such as Easter and Christmas]. He must offer Mass for his diocese on Sundays and major feast days. Every five years, the bishop must submit a report on the state of his diocese to the Pope.[28]

Each diocese is divided into individual parishes, each overseen by a priest. The parishes in a sense form the base of the pyramid of which the pope occupies the topmost position.

Choosing a New Pope

It has been established that the cardinals place the pope in that lofty position by choosing him from among their own ranks. But it was not always this way. In the Church's early centuries, local clergy and town officials who lived in Rome and its surrounding regions chose the popes. This process, however, was indecisive and often resulted in corruption, since the officials with the most influence usually got their way and thereby advanced their personal agendas.

The situation changed somewhat in 1059 when Pope Nicholas II made it a rule that only cardinals could choose the new pope. But some cardinals were more powerful than others and usually dominated the process. So in 1179 Pope Alexander III ordained that the cardinals who elected the popes had to have equal say and equal votes. About a century later, in 1274, Pope Gregory X introduced the now familiar custom of the cardinals holding the papal election in a secret meeting following the death of a reigning pope.

Other details of the papal election process were altered or added over time until about 1600, when that process assumed the approximate shape it bears today. When a pope dies (as in the case of John Paul II in 2005), the leader of the College of Cardinals calls a meeting of all members under the age of eighty, which must take place no more than twenty days later. At the meeting, the cardinals draw random lots to choose nine election officials. Of these, three distribute the voting ballots, three count the votes, and three review the results to make sure the rules have been followed. Upon receiving his ballot, each cardinal writes the name of the cardinal he would like to see become the new pontiff. The voter then carries the ballot to an altar and deposits it into a special container. When the votes are counted it takes a two-thirds

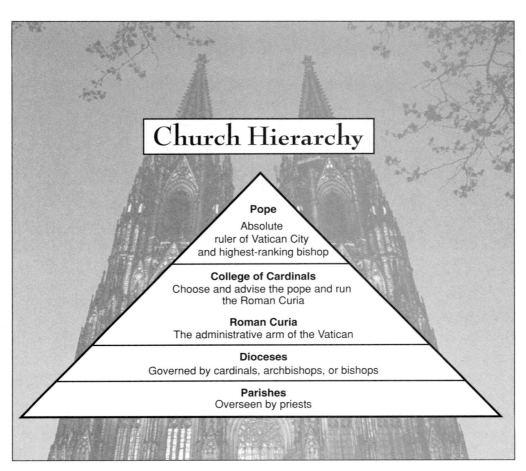

Church Hierarchy

Pope
Absolute
ruler of Vatican City
and highest-ranking bishop

College of Cardinals
Choose and advise the pope and run
the Roman Curia

Roman Curia
The administrative arm of the Vatican

Dioceses
Governed by cardinals, archbishops, or bishops

Parishes
Overseen by priests

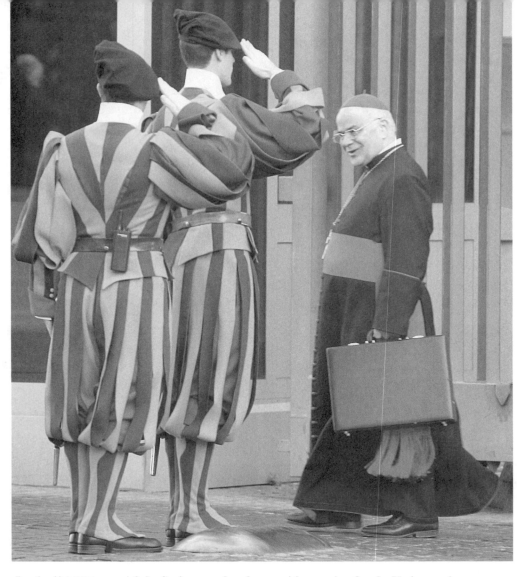

In April 2005, two of the Swiss guards who provide security for the Vatican salute a cardinal on his way to vote for a new pope.

majority to elect a pope. So if less than two-thirds of the cardinals vote for the same man, there must be another ballot. When someone is finally chosen, the oldest cardinal goes to the balcony of the Vatican Palace and, as happened in 2005 with Benedict XVI, announces to the waiting crowds "Habemus Papam!" This is Latin for "We have a pope!"

The Question of Papal Infallibility

Having been elected by the cardinals, the new pope immediately makes an appearance on the same balcony and blesses the faithful. Today, thanks to the existence of television, newspapers, and other mass media, that event flashes almost instantly to Catholics and others around the world. Later, a coronation ceremony takes place in which the nominee is officially crowned pope. In an unusual move, Pope John Paul II refused his coronation, apparently to emphasize his humble beginnings as the son of a Polish army officer.

But John Paul did not renounce his papal infallibility. Many Catholics believe the pope is infallible, or incapable of error, in matters of faith or morals (although it is thought that he can make mistakes in earthly matters). This doctrine of infallibility dates back to an eccentric fourteenth-century Franciscan monk, Petrus Olivi, who wanted to strengthen the papal office. In 1324 Pope John XXII condemned the idea as the work of the devil. But in 1870 Pope Pius IX pushed for its revival at a major Church council meeting, and, despite strenuous objections from many cardinals, the resolution passed.

Pope Pius IX's successor, Pope Leo XIII, had been one of these dissenters, so he did not lay claim to being infallible. However, most later popes accepted the doctrine. Still, it remains controversial, both inside and outside of the Church. Those who accept it often cite certain biblical passages that they say proves it, including one from the Gospel of Matthew in which Jesus told his disciples: "All authority in heaven and on Earth has been given to me. Go, therefore, and make disciples of all nations . . . teaching them to observe all that I have commanded you."[29] Supposedly, the popes are part of an unbroken line of teachers that began with Jesus, and because Jesus's spiritual teachings were infallible, those of the popes must be infallible as well.

But a number of influential Catholics, as well as ordinary members of the faith, reject this argument. A 1992 survey of Catholics aged fifteen to twenty-five taken in twelve countries, including the United States, found that 37 percent rejected the doctrine of papal infallibility, 37 percent accepted it, and 26 percent were unsure. Surveys also show that, regardless of whether or not they think the pope is infallible, the vast majority of Catholics recognize him as their spiritual leader and see the papacy as an integral and essential element of the faith.

chapter | five

Fundamental Catholic Beliefs and Practices

Like all religious faiths, Catholicism has a complex set of basic beliefs and various traditional acts of worship—practices that express or celebrate those beliefs. A few of these beliefs and practices existed right from the start, when the earliest Christians were still Jews trying to convince other Jews that Jesus was the Jewish Messiah. For example, the earliest believers already accepted that a single, all-powerful God had created the universe (since this was a long-held Jewish belief) and that Jesus had risen from the dead and ascended into heaven. The early Christians also celebrated Holy Communion in imitation of the consumption of bread and wine during the Last Supper, the meal Jesus shared with his disciples shortly before his death.

In contrast, many other now basic Catholic beliefs and practices developed or were introduced over time. A number of elements of the central ceremony of worship—the Mass—were added over the course of many centuries, for instance. And most of the Church's beliefs about original sin and its relation to salvation were added by the fifth-century Roman Christian thinker Augustine. Indeed, Catholic practices still undergo change from time to time.

One of the biggest changes in the twentieth century was allowing the traditional words of the Mass to be recited in the vernacular (the everyday language of those attending the ceremony) rather than Latin. This made the Mass more accessible to ordinary parishioners, most of whom were not fluent in Latin.

God and His Relationship with Humanity

A number of central Catholic beliefs and practices have changed very little or not at all since they were introduced. Among these core tenets of the faith are those dealing with the nature of God and his relationship with humanity and human communities. Some of these beliefs were inherited from Judaism, partly through Catholicism's acceptance of the Hebrew scriptures as the Old Testament (the first half of the Christian Bible). Other core Catholic beliefs derive from the New Testament (including the Gospels and writings of various early Christians) or from the writings, teachings, or decrees of leading Catholic thinkers and popes.

Regarding God's nature, the most basic Catholic belief is that of the Holy Trinity. A trinity is a group of three, and in this case the three elements are aspects of God's character—

This fifteenth-century painting depicts Augustine, the fifth-century theologian who defined many of the Church's ideas about original sin.

The Original Baptism

The sacrament of baptism, intended to introduce a person into the fellowship of the Church, has its original precedent in the baptism of Jesus by the itinerant Jewish preacher John the Baptist. According to the Gospel of Matthew, John met Jesus by the edge of the Jordan River.

In those days came John the Baptist, preaching in the wilderness of Judaea, "Repent, for the kingdom of heaven is at hand." For this is he who was spoken of by the prophet Isaiah when he said, "The voice of one crying in the wilderness: Prepare the way of the Lord, make his paths straight." . . . Then went out to him [Jews from] Jerusalem and all Judaea and all the region about the Jordan, confessing their sins. . . . Then Jesus came from Galilee to the Jordan to John, to be baptized by him. John would have prevented him, saying, "I need to be baptized by you, and do you come to me?" But Jesus answered him, "Let it be so now; for thus it is fitting for us to fulfill all righteousness." Then he consented. And when Jesus was baptized, he went up immediately from the water, and behold, the heavens opened and he saw the Spirit of God descending like a dove, and alighting on him; and lo, a voice from heaven, saying, "This is my beloved Son, with whom I am well pleased."

the Father, the Son, and the Holy Spirit. Catholics do not envision these as separate deities but, rather, as varying manifestations of the same God. Church leaders routinely admit that this concept is not easy to grasp, and accordingly, they often refer to the Trinity as one of the "mysteries" of the faith. (Official Church writings define a mystery as something that is "hidden in God, which can never be known unless . . . revealed by God."[30] Regarding this mystery, "it is not at all surprising that human attempts to understand God should stretch the human mind as far as it can go," Keith Ward writes.

It should not be forgotten that the idea of the Trinity is basically very simple. [Catholics] worship God as the creator of the universe. . . . [They also] worship God as one who enters into the universe, especially in the person of Jesus, to liberate persons from hatred and greed and lead them to eternal life. [In addition, they] worship God as the Spirit who inspires, guides, and strengthens the hearts and minds of created persons.[31]

As Ward points out, Catholics believe that God, in his manifestation as the Father, created the universe. They also believe that God created humanity. God is pictured as possessing the quality of truth and infinite amounts of love, and he is said to desire to share these things with the humans he created. He does so by revealing his expectations of people in the scriptures and elsewhere, and the way that people respond to these revelations is up to them. Catholicism teaches that God gave humans free will but that he wants them to use this gift wisely, by making good, moral choices in life.

Not everyone makes the right choices, however. Some people fall into sin, for which the Bible provides a precedent—the famous story of the first man and woman, Adam and Eve, in the Garden of Eden. God forbade them from eating fruit

This is one of many paintings depicting Adam and Eve in the Garden of Eden. According to the Bible, they sinned and God expelled them from Eden.

from a certain tree and they disobeyed him. This became known as the original sin. Following the ideas of Augustine, Catholicism teaches that all human beings have been tainted by it and must perform various rituals (especially baptism) to cleanse themselves of it.

The desire to rid humanity of sin was also behind Jesus Christ's mission to the world, Catholics believe. The part of the Trinity called the Son took human form on Earth in the person of Jesus, a phenomenon called the incarnation. The most crucial aspects of the incarnation were Jesus's suffering, death, and resurrection. "Jesus became a man to save men by reconciling them with God," Catholic writers Helen Keeler and Susan Grimbly explain.

> Jesus had to suffer and die so that mankind could be saved. Jesus's death was part of God's plan, long foretold by the Scriptures. ...Jesus took on man's sin and the suffering attached to it....He offered his life to the Father for [humanity's] sins, out of pure love. ...His death was the sacrifice ... which helped

restore man to communion with God.[32]

Catholic Views of Death and the Afterlife

Catholics hold that Jesus's resurrection also provided humans with a

Jesus rises from the dead in this painting. Catholics believe that his sacrifice made it possible for all humans to receive salvation after death.

potential path to salvation. The Church defines salvation as the process by which people overcome sin and their personal flaws and achieve a state of spirituality. In particular, following the death of one's earthly body, a person can achieve ultimate salvation when one's soul, or immaterial spirit, ascends into heaven. In this way, Catholicism teaches, death can be a gateway to everlasting life.

This assumes, of course, that the person is worthy. At the moment of death, Church doctrine says, God judges each individual. He reviews their lives and the deeds they performed and decides whether or not they deserve to be allowed to enter heaven. One of the chief examples cited by clergy in this regard is a passage from the Gospel of Luke, which begins:

> There was a rich man, who was clothed in purple [a color symbolizing royalty in ancient times] and fine linen, and who feasted sumptuously every day. And at his gate lay a poor man . . . full of sores, who desired to be fed with what fell from the rich man's table.[33]

The passage goes on to tell how, when the poor man died, he went to heaven. But the rich man, evidently because he did not make an effort to better the poor man's condition, was excluded from heaven.

How do Catholics envision heaven? This is difficult to answer because different people, theologians and ordinary persons alike, see heaven in different ways. Some have made the assumption that heaven is much like Earth—that is, with land, seas, mountains, and sky—only much more beautiful and free from crimes, disease, and despair. Others have expressed a less specific view of heaven, saying that it is too mysterious for humans to comprehend. But no matter how Catholics envision the physical conditions of heaven, they are universal in their belief that there they will meet God. This ability to see and know God and his glory and love is called "beatific vision." In heaven, Augustine wrote in his masterpiece *The City of God*,

> we shall rest and see, see and love, love and praise. This is what shall be in the end without end. For what other end do we propose to ourselves than to attain to the kingdom [of heaven] of which there is no end?[34]

As for those, like the rich man in the passage from Luke, who are excluded from heaven, their destinations following death can vary. Some, the Church preaches, go to purgatory. This is a sort of way station on the road to heaven. It is inhabited by the souls of people who had believed in God during their earthly lives but had committed some kind of sin. In purgatory, they receive punishment for said sin in order to purify them. Catholics believe that prayers from the living can help speed the souls in purgatory in their journey toward heaven.

According to Church doctrine, those Catholics who refuse to repent their sins, and also unbelievers, end up in hell after they die. Like heaven and purgatory, hell is often described in widely differing ways. A few people still describe it in graphic terms, picturing souls burning in eternal fires or undergoing gruesome tortures. However, most Catholics, including the vast majority of priests and other clergy, have come to view hell as another mystery of the faith. So they tend to describe it in vaguer terms. Among the more popular views are that hell consists of having to endure the absence of God forever—presumably a terrible fate for a person's soul to suffer—or the complete destruction of the soul, resulting in a state of nonexistence.

Liturgy and the Catholic Mass

Catholics express and celebrate their beliefs in a wide range of traditional and often colorful rituals. Collectively, these acts of worship are referred to as the liturgy. Most aspects of the liturgy do not appear in the Bible but developed and underwent modifications over time through practice and acceptance by Church leaders. For example, in the council known as Vatican II, held in the 1960s, the pope and other high-ranking clergy made a number of minor changes in the liturgy, and there is little doubt that other alterations will be made in the future.

The central liturgical service in Catholicism is the Mass. The most familiar Mass is the one held every Sunday in all Catholic churches. However, more elaborate versions, called High Masses, are held on special feast days (such as Easter), and local priests often hold a small-scale Mass on a daily basis.

The average Mass opens with introductory rites that are sometimes called the "liturgy of the word" because the priest conducting the ceremony speaks God's words to the congregation. These words take the form of short readings from the Bible. Usually the first one is from the Old Testament and the second from the New Testament. At the conclusion of the readings the priest says "Alleluia," at which point the worshippers traditionally stand. Then the priest and worshippers recite the Nicene Creed.

First adopted by bishops in the fourth century, this is a brief list of core Catholic beliefs. Following is an excerpt from the Creed:

> We believe in one God, the Father, the Almighty, maker of heaven and earth, of all that is seen and unseen. We believe in one Lord, Jesus Christ, the only Son of God. . . . For our salvation he came down from heaven: by the power of the Holy Spirit he was born of the Virgin Mary, and became man. . . . He was crucified . . . and was buried. On the third day he rose again . . . he ascended into heaven and is seated at the right hand of the Father. He will come again in glory to judge the living and the dead.[35]

The next—and principal—part of the Mass is concerned with the Eucharist, or union with Christ. (The term *Eucharist* comes from the Greek words *eukharistos*, meaning "thankful," and *kharis*, meaning "grace.") The Eucharist has several other names, perhaps the most common being Holy Communion. In imitation of the events of the Last Supper, the worshippers drink a sip of wine, which symbolizes Christ's blood, and eat a bite of bread (usually in the form of a wafer), which stands for Christ's body. The Church teaches that during the Mass the bread and wine are converted into

Background of the Nicene Creed

The Nicene Creed, now a standard part of the Catholic Mass, dates back to the fourth century. At the time, a splinter group of Christians—the Arians—suggested that Jesus and God were not one and the same. Rather, they were separate beings and God was somewhat superior to Jesus. This provoked great debate and conflict among the Roman Catholic bishops and thinkers of the day. To address the issue, the emperor Constantine called a great council in 325 at Nicaea, in Asia Minor (what is now Turkey), an event attended by more than two hundred bishops. The majority, backed by the emperor, rejected the Arians' argument and adopted the concept of *homoousio*, "of the same substance," essentially meaning that Jesus and God were one and the same. They also formulated a creed designed to clarify the "proper" way of viewing God and Jesus. With a few later additions, it became known as the Nicene Creed (after Nicaea).

An Italian priest administers Holy Communion. The wafer he holds stands for Christ's body. The rite also features wine, symbolizing Christ's blood.

Christ's flesh and blood (a process called transubstantiation). According to Catholic doctrine, Communion draws worshippers closer to both Christ and the Church and helps to obtain God's graces. After Holy Communion has been completed, the priest generally says a prayer and then blesses and dismisses the worshippers, concluding the Mass.

The Seven Sacraments

The Eucharist is one of the seven central examples of Catholic liturgy, known as the sacraments. The other six are baptism, confirmation, penance, anointing the sick, marriage, and holy orders. Catholics see the sacraments as rituals that bring a person closer to Christ and the Church at important moments in his or her life. The sacraments are intended to instruct people about Catholic beliefs and to renew and strengthen their personal faith in those beliefs.

Three of the sacraments—baptism, confirmation, and the Eucharist—are sometimes collectively called the "sacraments of initiation." The idea of being initiated is most evident in baptism because it is through this act—immersing in or sprinkling with water—that a person first gains entry into the Church. "The water is symbolic of death and rebirth," Keeler and Grimbly explain.

The baptized person dies in the water and is reborn in Christ, just as Christ himself died on the cross and was resurrected. The waters of baptism have a cleansing effect, as the soul of the baptized person is washed and renewed by the Holy Spirit.[36]

The second sacrament, confirmation, is thought to be a sort of completion of the initiation begun in baptism. The confirmation ceremony consists of a bishop applying holy oil (called chrism) to the worshipper's forehead. Most Catholics receive confirmation in their midteens, though a person can receive it at any age.

Two other sacraments are sometimes called the "sacraments of healing." One, penance—also called confession—consists of a worshipper first admitting to having committed a sin and then seeking forgiveness for it. Most often, the worshipper enters a small chamber called the confessional, where a priest hears the confession. The priest usually forgives him or her in hopes that the sin will not be repeated. The other healing sacrament, anointing the sick, draws on the stories of Jesus and his disciples helping ill and afflicted people. "In my name," Jesus says in the Gospel of Mark, those "who believe [in me] will lay their hands on the sick."[37] Essentially, this sacrament

The Stations of the Cross

One of the more colorful aspects of Catholic liturgy is called the stations of the cross. It began during the Crusades when religious pilgrims visiting Jerusalem attempted to retrace the Via Dolorosa, the route Jesus took through the city to the place he was crucified. The pilgrims noted fourteen milestones, or stations, in this journey, including the place where the Roman governor sentenced Jesus to death; three points where Jesus supposedly fell while carrying his cross; the place where he encountered his mother, Mary; the place where he was nailed to the cross; and the location of his tomb. Today, many Catholic churches feature a series of fourteen pictures, plaques, or other dedications set up on the inside walls, each representing one of the stations of the cross. A worshipper can walk from station to station, saying a brief prayer at each stop, in effect showing respect for Jesus's sacrifice.

Because marriage is one of the sacraments of the Church, most Catholics get married in a church.

hoped that the patient will recover.

The last two sacraments —marriage and holy orders —are sometimes called the "sacraments of commitment." This is because a long-term commitment by the participants is expected. The marriage sacrament is based on the belief that God created humans out of love and therefore he calls on men and women to love each other and blesses their union as man and wife. In the sacrament of holy orders, a man (since women are not allowed to take part) is ordained a minister of the Catholic Church —a deacon, a priest, or a bishop. The ceremony must be performed by a bishop and the candidate has to have been previously baptized.

Other Important Catholic Practices

Besides the Mass and sacraments, Catholics engage in numerous other devotional practices and observances. Prayers are perhaps the most common. They can be of any length and content and recit-

consists of a priest anointing a gravely ill person with oil to prepare that person for death and the journey to heaven, although it is always

ed at any given moment, but over time a number of special Catholic prayers evolved. The most familiar is the "Our Father," which is said during Mass. Another kind of prayer—the novena—is recited for nine days in a row by one person to aid another person who is sick or in trouble. And a rosary is a prayer intended to express devotion to Jesus's mother, Mary.

Still other aspects of the liturgy include the use of standard substances and objects. These include holy water in baptisms and other ceremonies; candles and incense to set the right mood for prayer, meditation, and spirituality; bells to announce the hour of a church service; the wearing of crucifixes (crosses) to indicate and rejoice in one's faith; and the preservation and veneration of holy relics, objects that once belonged to saints or other persons deemed holy by the Church. These materials, along with the Mass and other time-honored liturgical practices, help Catholics maintain both a connection with their roots and a sense of tradition and stability in a rapidly changing world.

chapter six

Reforms Bring the Church into the Modern Era

If a Catholic born in the 1700s or early 1800s had been able to construct a time machine and travel to the present day, he or she would almost certainly be shocked at the changes undergone by the Church in a relatively short span of time. But modern Catholics would no doubt tell the time traveler that these changes had been necessary. Otherwise, the Church might well have lost its relevance and authority in a world shaped by rapidly evolving technology and new social and political ideas. When the Reformation, scientific revolution, Enlightenment, and democratic movements swept Europe in early modern times, the Catholic Church at first tried to resist. But it eventually became clear that this approach was futile. As Keeler and Grimbly put it:

> The demise of monarchies and the rise of democratically elected governments throughout Europe undermined some of the protections that Catholic churches had enjoyed. Liberalism and freethinking, which were replacing blind obedience to authority, challenged the individual's adherence to the Church. Society was becoming more liberal, less dogmatic, more freethinking, and more secular. As a

result, the Catholic Church came to be associated with the old world order, and some governments even adopted an anti-Catholic stand. Many individuals lost their belief in God ... [and] by the middle of the nineteenth century, Catholics in Europe were a fractured and insecure group.[38]

In the face of this onrush of the forces of modernism, it became clear to Church leaders that something had to be done. The first major attempt to institute reforms was the council known as Vatican I, which began in 1869. Though hopes were at first high, many Catholics, clergy and laypersons (ordinary Catholics) alike, were disappointed when the council devoted most of its time to the issue of the pope's infallibility. Political events in Europe forced the meeting to adjourn before any substantive reforms could be debated.

Real reforms did come in the twentieth century. Pope Leo XIII (reigned 1878–1903) and Pope Pius X (1903–1914) instituted some minor ones. But much more systemic and far-reaching reforms were enacted under the council known as Vatican II,

Pope John XXIII greets throngs of well-wishers in St. Peter's Square in 1960. The reform-minded Vatican II council began its work during his reign.

which began in 1962, when John XXIII was pope. "There was a new, fundamentally positive attitude to modern progress," recalls Hans Kung, who played an active role in the council, "and to the secular world, science, and democracy generally." The Church "clearly disassociated itself from [its former image] as a kind of supernatural Roman Empire" and replaced it with the image of "a fellowship of faith which is constantly on the way in the world, a sinful and provisional pilgrim folk, ready for ever-new reform."[39]

A More User-Friendly Church?

Some of the reforms enacted in the twentieth century were logistical—that is, they dealt with the structure of the Church and how it operates. In effect, these changes made the Church more user-friendly, not only for ordinary Catholics but for the clergy at all levels. One important aspect of this process was an earnest effort to partially decentralize the Church's traditional hierarchy of power. Under the new system, the pope and cardinals remained the major leaders of the faith; however, the individual bishops were given a larger role in Church policy.

For example, more than two thousand bishops voted at Vatican

II and thereby shaped all the new policies adopted. The bishops were also encouraged to meet among themselves on a regular basis in their respective regions. The idea was to encourage both a discussion of local issues and problems and the enactment of reforms on the local level where appropriate. In these ways, the Church showed a willingness to retreat somewhat from the long-standing policy in which any and all reform had to come from papal directives.

More authority was also given to laypersons, who were allowed and encouraged to play larger roles in their churches. This was reflected in the title of the Vatican II directive in question—the *Apostolicam Actuositatem*, Latin for "apostle-like activity." In fact, the directive acknowledged that laypersons can, like Jesus's apostles did, actively work to better the Church and spread the Catholic faith. The directive indicated that they would do this by aiding their local priests and bishops in a sort of partnership of the faithful:

As sharers in the role of Christ as priest, prophet, and king, the laity have their work cut out for them in the life and activity of the Church. Their activity is so necessary within the Church com-

A layperson administers Communion to a worshipper in New York City in 2001. As a result of Vatican II, laypersons play larger roles in Church activities.

munities that without it the [clergy is] often unable to achieve its full effectiveness. In the manner of the men and women who helped Paul in spreading the Gospel ... the laity with the right apostolic attitude supply what is lacking to their brethren and refresh the spirit of pastors and of the rest of the faithful. ... Strengthened by active participation in the liturgical life of their community, they ... [can] offer their special skills to make the care of souls and the administration of ... the Church more efficient and effective. ... As far as possible the laity ought to provide helpful collaboration for every apostolic and missionary undertaking sponsored by their local parish.[40]

Another way the Church's hierarchy recognized the needs of Catholic laypersons was to allow them to conduct most aspects of the liturgy in their own languages.

In the same spirit of respect and brotherhood, Church leaders also reached out beyond Catholic membership to Protestants and other non-Catholics. Ever since the Reformation, the Church's official policy had been that Protestants were misguided persons that must be converted back to Catholicism. But in Vatican II, the Church finally recognized their non-Catholic Christian brethren. The Church went so far as to admit that in the past it had contributed to Christian disunity and now committed itself to uniting all Christians in a spirit of toleration and friendship.

Reconciliation with the Jews

This gesture of admitting to a past mistake was not an isolated case. In fact, such admissions became part of the modernizing transformation the Church underwent in the twentieth century. Perhaps the most striking example was the way several popes, as well as the Church itself, reached out to Jews. The relationship between Catholicism and Judaism had long been strained. Throughout ancient and medieval times, Catholics routinely and irrationally blamed the Jews—all Jews, past, present, and future—for Jesus's death. And like most other Europeans, Catholics had marginalized Jews by forcing them to live in squalid ghettos. In fact, a 1555 papal decree had confined Rome's Jews to a swamp-ridden ghetto in that city. Any Jews who ventured outside the ghetto had to wear yellow caps to identify themselves as Jews.

The modern Catholic reconciliation with Jews began under Pope John XXIII, who stated publicly that it was an error to blame the Jews as a people—in either the past or present—for Jesus's death. This new attitude was debated and became part of official Church policy during Vatican II. One of the written directives—the *Nostra Aetate*, meaning "in our time"—addressed Church relations with non-Christians, especially Muslims and Jews. The bishops voted by the overwhelming margin of 2,221 to 88 to accept the following teachings: "The Apostles, the Church's main-stay and pillars . . . sprang from the Jewish people. . . . What happened in His passion [sufferings and death] cannot be charged against all the Jews, without distinction, then alive, nor against the Jews of today . . . [and the Church condemns] hatred, persecutions, [and] displays of anti-Semitism, directed against Jews at any time and by anyone."[41]

Between Catholics and Jews

The Vatican II Council issued a number of directives, among them one (quoted in "Documents of the Vatican II Council") that stated the following about the special relationship between Catholicism and Judaism.

The Church of Christ acknowledges that, according to God's saving design, the beginnings of her faith and her election are found already among the [Jewish] Patriarchs, Moses, and the [Jewish] prophets. . . . The Church, therefore, cannot forget that she received the revelation of the Old Testament through the people [the Jews] with whom God in His inexpressible mercy concluded the Ancient Covenant. . . . Indeed, the Church believes that by His cross Christ, Our Peace, reconciled Jews and Gentiles, making both one in Himself. . . . She also recalls that the Apostles, the Church's main-stay and pillars, as well as most of the early disciples who proclaimed Christ's Gospel to the world, sprang from the Jewish people. . . . The Jews should not be presented as rejected or accursed by God, as if this followed from the Holy Scriptures. All should see to it, then, that in catechetical work or in the preaching of the word of God they do not teach anything that does not conform to the truth of the Gospel and the spirit of Christ. Furthermore, in her rejection of every persecution against any man, the Church . . . [rejects] hatred, persecutions, displays of anti-Semitism, directed against Jews at any time and by anyone.

Though in Vatican II the Church took an important step toward reconciling with the Jews, it was Pope John Paul II who eventually transformed written policy and verbal statements into concrete action. Incredibly, before his papacy not one of his predecessors had ever set foot in a Jewish synagogue. In John Paul's view, this was sad and just plain wrong. So in 1986 he asked Elio Toaff, then the chief rabbi of Rome, if he would mind a papal visit to his synagogue. Shocked but happy, Toaff quickly assented. The historic moment came on April 13 of that year. "He [John Paul] was followed by bishops, and I was followed by rabbis," Toaff later recalled. "And he hugged me as if I were family. In his speech, everyone felt his love, his affection. He made a tie between Judaism and Christianity and, in doing so, he found a way to move us all."[42] John Paul went even further later. In a visit to Jewish holy sites in Jerusalem in

Pope John Paul II admires the ceiling of the synagogue in Rome during his historic 1986 visit, part of an effort to reconcile with the Jews.

2000, he delivered a message expressing deep regret for past Catholic persecutions of Jews.

Confronting Scientific Reality

Another past error that John Paul courageously acknowledged and apologized for involved perhaps the most infamous incident in the Church's long series of battles with science. The trial and condemnation of Galileo in the early seventeenth century had long been an unhealed black eye for Catholicism. It had also become a symbol of the Church's routine resistance to any new scientific ideas that seemed to challenge traditional Catholic doctrine. In the twentieth century a number of Catholic leaders, including John Paul, recognized the need for the Church to break a harmful pattern. "The scientific discovery of a theory is announced, and theologians react defensively," Catholic clergyman Jerome Langford points out. "Usually by the time theologians get around to accepting a scientific discovery, they are years behind the times."[43] This repeated policy had often left the Church open to ridicule and contributed to its "old world" image.

John Paul saw that this was particularly true in the case of Galileo and the heliocentric theory. By 1700, all scientists, including those who were priests, had accepted the reality that Earth moves around the sun. Yet the Church did not lift its ban on books discussing the heliocentric theory until 1822. Moreover, as late as the 1980s, no pope or other high Church official had ever apologized for the shameful way the Church had treated Galileo.

In an effort to rectify this situation, in October 1992 John Paul formally acknowledged the mistakes the Church had made in Galileo's case. At the time, he said, Church authorities had interpreted the scriptures too literally, which had unfortunately led them to reject certain scientific realities. John Paul

The Pope Admits That Galileo Was Right

In the early 1990s, Pope John Paul II, quoted here from the November 4, 1992, issue of L'Osservatore Romano, *apologized for the Church's poor treatment of the great Italian scientist Galileo and admitted that the Church had been wrong in its rejection of the heliocentric theory.*

The problem posed by theologians of that age was the compatibility between heliocentrism and Scripture. Thus the new science, with its methods and the freedom of research which they implied, obliged theologians to examine their own criteria of scriptural interpretation. Most of them did not know how to do so. Paradoxically, Galileo, a sincere believer, showed himself to be more perceptive in this regard than the theologians who opposed him. "If Scripture cannot err," he [said], "certain of its interpreters and commentators can and do so in many ways." . . . The majority of theologians did not recognize the formal distinction between Sacred Scripture and its interpretation, and this led them unduly to transpose into the realm of the doctrine of the faith a question which in fact pertained to scientific investigation.

The Church issued a formal apology to Galileo in 1992.

also emphasized the urgent need for the Church to avoid such mistakes in the future. Confrontations between science and religious faith can be avoided in part, he said, by accepting that they are two distinct disciplines, each earnestly seeking to discover fundamental truths about the universe. These disciplines sometimes meet at "points of contact" and should respect each other, he added. That way they can both remain viable and meaningful. "From the Galileo affair," John Paul said,

The Church generally accepts Darwin's theory of evolution, although it holds that God set evolution in motion.

we can learn a lesson which remains valid in relation to similar situations which occur today and which may occur in the future. . . . Different branches of knowledge call for different methods. . . . The distinction between the two realms of knowledge ought not to be understood as opposition. The two realms are not altogether foreign to each other, [but] have points of contact. The methodologies proper to each make it possible to bring out different aspects of reality.[44]

God Created Science?

The main thrust of John Paul's apology in the Galileo case seemed to be

that two realms of knowledge—one scientifically based, the other spiritually based—can coexist and find areas of agreement. This was certainly the way that John Paul and other twentieth-century popes, along with many Catholic theologians in that era, approached the controversy of evolution. English biologist Charles Darwin had created a stir in both scientific and religious circles with his 1859 publication of *The Origin of Species*. But within a generation, virtually all reputable scientists had accepted the basic tenets of his theory that species of plants and animals change and develop over time. And nearly all of the major scientific discoveries of the twentieth century confirmed that Darwin was right.

Numerous modern Church leaders and thinkers refrained from rejecting the theory of evolution outright, as their predecessors had rejected the heliocentric theory. Instead, the Church came to an accommodation with science on the evolution question. That synthesis of scientific and Catholic doctrine is referred to as "the-istic evolution" or "developmental creation." First, modern Catholicism accepts that the universe may be very old and that it may have developed into its present state over long time periods. However, the Church maintains, this process was set in motion and guided by God. Second, biological evolution, as described by Darwin and others, may well have occurred. But if so, it too was initiated and/or overseen by God.

The Church views human beings as a special case within biological evolution. Pope Pius XII, John Paul II,

Pius XII Addresses Evolution

Among the writings of Pope Pius XII was a 1950 statement, the Humani Generi *(quoted here from "Encyclicals of Pius XII"), which addressed Catholic views of the scientific theory of evolution. The main thrust of the text was that considering the doctrine of evolution is all right for Catholics, as long as they recognize that human souls are specially created by God.*

The Church does not forbid that, in conformity with the present state of human sciences and sacred theology, research and discussions, on the part of men experienced in both fields, take place with regard to the doctrine of evolution, in as far as it inquires into the origin of the human body as coming from pre-existent and living matter, for the Catholic faith obliges us to hold that souls are immediately created by God. However, this must be done in such a way that the reasons for both opinions, that is, those favorable and those unfavorable to evolution, be weighed and judged with the necessary seriousness, moderation and measure, and provided that all are prepared to submit to the judgment of the Church, to whom Christ has given the mission of interpreting authentically the Sacred Scriptures and of defending the dogmas of faith.

and other modern Catholic leaders have agreed that the body and soul must be viewed as separate entities with separate origins. Thus, while the human physical form may have developed over time, the human soul was separately and specially created by God. "The Church does not forbid . . . research and discussions . . . [about] evolution," Pius stated. But "the Catholic faith obliges us to hold that souls are immediately created by God."[45]

In this way, the Church has managed to keep itself abreast of current scientific knowledge and at the same time remain a relevant, influential force in a world dominated by scientific progress. In essence, Catholicism has reconciled itself with science by adopting the view that God created the major scientific principles and processes that human beings discover and observe. Therefore, science and Catholic faith are perfectly compatible; moreover, God seems all the more impressive for his foresight in designing nature's complex, interactive physical system. In the words of the recently revised official catechism (book of religious instruction) of the Catholic Church:

> The question about the origins of the world and of man has been the object of many scientific studies which have splendidly enriched our knowledge of the age and dimensions of the cosmos, the development of life-forms and the appearance of man. These discoveries invite us to even greater admiration for the greatness of the Creator, prompting us to give him thanks for all his works and for the understanding and wisdom he gives to scholars and researchers.[46]

The Church as a Political Force

Still another way the Catholic Church met the problems of the modern world head-on was by taking stands on crucial political issues. This not only gave it more relevancy in society as a whole but also made the Church a potent force for political change. Among the issues Church leaders weighed in on were the role of the United States in Latin America; economic justice for the poor; health care and child welfare; and human rights.

Perhaps Catholicism's biggest recent political risk was also its greatest single political success. This was the stand taken by Pope John Paul II against communism, which many historians believe was a major factor in the collapse of the Soviet Union in the early 1990s. John Paul had grown up in Soviet-dominated Poland and had

John Paul II visits his native Poland in 1979. His courageous stand against communism was a major factor in the collapse of the Soviet Union.

long opposed the Communist system there. After becoming pope, he courageously brought the considerable influence of his office to bear against that oppressive system. Beginning in June 1979, John Paul made a series of visits to his native land. He rallied the Polish workers, most of whom were Catholic, and inspired them to demand better working and living conditions. The result was a labor organization that grew into a full-fledged democracy movement, which in turn inspired resistance against the Communist system in other countries. After the Soviet Union's fall, former Russian leader Mikhail Gorbachev admitted: "What has happened in Eastern Europe in recent years would not have been possible without the presence of this Pope, without the great role, even political, that he has played on the world scene."[47]

Indeed, John Paul and a few other twentieth-century popes had helped the Church come of age in the modern world and recapture some of the relevancy and stature it had lost in previous centuries. The question is whether this stature can be maintained in the twenty-first century. In the wake of a new series of internal problems and scandals, a number of Catholics worry about the Church's image and urge its leaders to continue the recent spirit of reform.

chapter|seven

The Twenty-First Century: New Demands for Reform

As Catholicism enters its third millennium, it faces a mix of blessings, problems, and challenges. On the one hand, the faith remains widespread, with hundreds of millions of devout and devoted members spread across the globe. And the pope is still one of the preeminent spiritual leaders in the world, respected and influential even among some non-Catholics. Meanwhile, Catholic missionaries do their best to spread the doctrines of their faith, and Catholic volunteers of all ages aid the poor, the sick, and the underprivileged in numerous third-world countries. "Active Catholic men and women all over the world . . . [untiringly] engage in social work," Kung writes. "They give us courage [and] the cause of the Church is alive."[48] These and other factors suggest that the Catholic Church has a bright future in the twenty-first century and beyond.

On the other hand, a number of leading Catholics predict that the Church's continued success will not be easy. This is partly because the faith has a great deal of competition in an increasingly diverse marketplace of religious and nonreligious ideas, disciplines, and lifestyles. Protestantism (especially its evangelical branches), Islam, Buddhism, and various other faiths vie with Catholicism for the hearts and minds of individuals. Or at least the existence of so many diverse religions forces members of each, including Catholicism, to question their own traditions. "We Americans," James Carroll points out,

> have discovered with something approaching astonishment the wild diversity of religious and spiritual impulses that has come to mark not only the planet, but also our own nation. . . . Even from within Catholicism, this new circumstance means the assumptions of every religion must now be the subject of reexamination.[49]

Another factor that competes with Catholicism, or at least works against maintaining traditional Catholic values, is modern materialism. The desire, or often the perceived need, to make more and more money to support expensive,

On Christmas day in 2003, nuns distribute food in Calcutta, India. Catholic clergy and laypersons alike aid the poor around the world.

comfortable lifestyles consumes increasing numbers of people, both Catholics and non-Catholics. This is especially true in industrialized, economically well-off countries like the United States. For large numbers of people in fast-paced, consumer-based, media-driven societies, churches, including the Catholic Church, often have to compete for the time and commitment of people with hectic schedules and limited attention spans.

Finally, and perhaps most important, the Church faces new charges of internal corruption, outmoded customs, and demands for a new round of reforms. In particular, the foundations of Catholicism were recently shaken by the realization that some priests had been molesting children. These charges resulted in a number of arrests and prosecutions of priests, as well as much bad publicity and financial woes for the Church (because of expensive lawsuits brought by the victims of the abuse). Meanwhile, increasingly large numbers of Catholics think that priests should be allowed to marry and that women should be allowed to become priests.

A Pressing Shortage of Priests

Some reform-minded Catholics believe that the fact that priests are not allowed to marry is a major factor behind one of the biggest chal-

Priest Shortages Affect Teachers and Schools

The ongoing shortage of priests has taken a heavy toll in Catholic elementary and high schools, in which many of the teachers had traditionally been priests. Typical have been the negative effects in Cincinnati, Ohio. In the 1960s, about 60 percent of the teachers in the city's Catholic schools were priests and nuns; today, that proportion is only 4 percent. Catholic laypeople now teach most of the classes in these schools, even the religion classes. "The impact has been far-reaching," report Denise S. Amos and Dan Horn (in a May 4, 2004, article for the *Cincinnati Enquirer*). "Catholic schools began charging—then raising—tuition to pay teacher salaries and benefits. Now most local Catholic elementary schools charge $1,000 to $2,000 a year, while most high schools charge double or triple that amount."

A shortage of priests in some areas of the world is one of the many challenges the Catholic Church presently faces.

lenges the Church presently faces. Namely, there is a serious shortage of priests, a problem that appears to be worsening as time goes on. In England, for instance, the number of Catholic priests fell from seven thousand in 1980 to fifty-five hundred in 2005. And more than half of the existing priests are older than sixty. In the United States, 27 percent of Catholic parishes have no resident priests, and enrollment in U.S. seminaries (which train new priests) is now half of what it was thirty years ago. One Canadian diocese has only eight priests to serve a total membership of some twenty thousand. The situation is even worse in countries such as Honduras, where there are only four hundred priests to serve 5 million Catholics.

A number of causes have been claimed for these shortages. Probably most often discussed is the official Church requirement that priests remain celibate and unmarried. In small Latin American nations, the celibacy requirement is the most common reason given by young men who are asked why they do not join the priesthood. Actually, the same reason has been cited in larger, wealthier countries by those priests who have quit the priesthood. In Cincinnati, Ohio, for example, Catholic priest Savio Russo eventually felt that his calling to raise a family was greater than his calling to be a priest. So he left the priesthood, married, and had children. Being a priest "was a pretty exciting life," he says, "but it was lonely."[50]

A number of reformers say that the shortage of priests could be alleviated, at least in part, by allowing priests to marry. They point out that the celibacy requirement is not a matter of doctrine—meaning that it is not written in the Bible as a rule handed down from God. In fact, married, sexually active priests were quite common in the Church until the First Lateran Council imposed the celibacy rule in 1123. Therefore, the reformers say, the rule could easily be changed by a papal directive. However, as one commentator puts it:

The church is not a democracy, and rewriting rules that have been in place for 800 years is no easy task. Any change in the celibacy rule would require the approval of the Vatican, which has shown little support for that move. The pope believes a priest can best serve his flock if he is solely devoted to his church, and not distracted by the demands of family life.[51]

How long the Vatican can maintain this position is an open question. A 1992 Gallup poll found that fully 75 percent of U.S. Catholics favor allowing priests to marry. And similar polls taken in other countries since that time have produced similar results. It is possible that the Catholic laity may eventually exert enough pressure to convince the Vatican to change its position on this issue.

Should Women Be Ordained?

The Vatican is much more resistant to change in a somewhat related area—namely, the ordination of women as priests. The two issues are related, reformers point out, because allowing women to become priests would help alleviate the growing shortage of priests. (The Church does allow women to become nuns. But nuns are limited to duties such as aiding the poor and teaching and are not allowed to conduct baptism, mass, or other sacraments. So they do not have the same status as priests within the Church hierarchy.)

Most popes and other high-ranking Church leaders have steadfastly rejected the ordination of women. One of their major arguments is that Jesus's apostles—in a sense his principal ministers—were all men.

Also, all of the leaders of the early Christian churches were men. If Jesus wanted women to be ministers of his word, the argument goes, he would have had female as well as male followers, and some of the early churches would have been run by women.

Those who support the ordination of women argue that Jesus did have a number of women followers. They cite Mary Magdalene, who

Paul on the Equality of Men and Women

One of the key arguments used by Catholic reformers who want to see women ordained as priests is this passage from Galatians (3:26–28), *in which the apostle Paul seems to call men and women equal in Jesus's eyes, and therefore, as the reformers see it, equally worthy to serve the faithful as priests.*

Through faith you are all children of God in Jesus Christ. For all of you who were baptized into Christ['s church] have clothed yourselves with Christ. There is neither Jew nor Greek, there is neither slave nor free person, there is not male and female. For you are all one in Jesus Christ.

St. Paul seemed to say that men and women are equal in Jesus's eyes.

often traveled with Jesus, as one. They also point out that, according to the Bible and other early Christian writings, the early Church had a number of deaconesses (female deacons) who ministered to the needs of both women and men. Indeed, in his letters the apostle Paul praised a number of women for their activities as religious organizers. One was a deaconess named Phoebe. Also singled out for praise were Priscilla, who established a church in her home in Rome, and Lydia, who did the same in Philippi, in Greece.

Another argument used by Church leaders against the ordination of women is that Jesus was a man and therefore cannot be adequately represented in Holy Communion and other sacred ceremonies by a woman. Furthermore, the popes and all ordained priests have always been men, in imitation of Jesus, a man. This tradition, which lies at the core of Catholicism, should be respected and maintained.

The counterargument is that women, like men, are made in God's image. Therefore, if it can be accepted that women have equal rights with men as human beings, it should follow that women can

serve equally well as priests. Furthermore, some reformers point out, the "tradition" argument against ordaining women as priests is invalid because such traditions were based on deep-seated prejudices against women that developed in the unenlightened cultures of ancient and medieval times. John Wijngaards, a leading Catholic

Protesters who advocate ordaining women picket bishops and archbishops on their way to a meeting in Chicago in June 2005.

reformer, writes that women have traditionally been excluded from the priesthood by definition—that is, simply for being women:

> Women were considered inferior by nature and by law. According to the Greek philosophy which was adopted also by Christians, women were thought to be inferior to men by nature. Roman law, which became the basis for the Church's laws, granted women a low status in society. . . . It was unthinkable that such "an inferior creature" could be ordained a priest. Women were considered to be in a state of punishment for sin. Women were held responsible for bringing original sin into the world, and for being a continuing source of seduction. . . . Women were considered ritually unclean. A woman's monthly flow of blood was supposed to put her regularly into a state of ritual defilement. Church leaders were anxious that such uncleanness might defile the holiness of the church building, the sanctuary, and mainly the altar. . . . It is clear that anyone who is under the influence of one of these prejudices, leave alone a combination of them, could not possibly entertain the idea of women's ordination![52]

A more modern prejudice frequently cited by the reformers is that the Church's all-male elite is too often out of touch with women. "While many parish priests develop an understanding of the problems of women's lives by ministering to women in their congregations," Keeler and Grimbly suggest, "those who rise highest in the Church are more isolated." Some say that this situation "leads to condescending and anti-feminist attitudes" and a lack of "discussion from a female point of view."[53] Leaders in the Church usually counter by pointing out that a majority of bishops, cardinals, and popes began as parish priests and therefore do understand the problems and needs of Catholic women.

A Betrayal of Trust

The shortage of priests, arguments over allowing priests to marry, and the ordination of women are important issues that concern and sometimes divide modern Catholics. But the attention given these issues in recent years, both inside and outside the Church, has paled in comparison to that given to a scandal that hit Catholicism, in Carroll's words, like "a tidal wave."[54] In the 1980s and 1990s, a number of Catholic priests in Ireland and other parts of Europe

Children are among the protesters outside a Boston cathedral in July 2003. The scandal involving child abuse by priests has rocked the Church.

as a significant factor in the drop in church attendance—from 63 to 48 percent—in Ireland's capital, Dublin, in the 1990s.

The sex scandal gained much broader coverage in the media after similar allegations of abuse were lodged against a number of U.S. priests and bishops beginning in the late 1990s. Matters became worse when an investigation launched by the *Boston Globe* newspaper revealed that high-ranking clergy had known about some of the abuses and engaged in a long-standing cover-up. According to the *Globe*, a victim of abuse by a local priest finally got up the nerve to tell the archbishop of Boston. The archbishop alleged-ly told the victim, "I bind you by the power of the confessional never to speak about this to anyone else."[55]

These and other aspects of the abuses and cover-up provoked wide-spread outrage among Catholics in the United States and elsewhere. Most Catholics accepted, and still accept, claims made by the Vatican and many archbishops and bishops that the abusers represent only a tiny percentage of Catholic clergy. Yet large numbers of parishioners were shocked that even a small proportion of priests had committed such crimes. The prevailing view is that the abusers betrayed both their flocks, who trust-

were accused of making sexual advances to or of sexually molesting male and female members of their congregations. One Irish clergyman was charged with abusing hundreds of young men between 1945 and 1990. These scandals are widely seen

ed them implicitly, and the Church itself. "The scandal led to an unprecedented explosion of Catholic awareness of Church failures," Carroll points out,

and a new climate of religious self-criticism has taken on a particularly pointed meaning among Catholics, especially lay people. . . . In parishes throughout the United States, Catholics gathered in large numbers to discuss a range of matters spilling over from the abuse crisis. As reports surfaced of financial settlements secretly paid to victims over the years, Catholic . . . foundations demanded an accounting of the

monies they donated to the Church, and parishioners began withholding contributions from collection baskets.[56]

Financial Woes

These are not the only financial woes produced by the sex abuse scandal. Various dioceses have had to pay out enormous sums of money to settle lawsuits brought by abuse victims. Late in 2003, the Boston archdiocese paid $85 million to five hundred victims, for example.

Some Catholic commentators have remarked that these huge payouts could not have come at a worse time. They say that even before the sex abuse scandal came to the fore,

Will Paying the Victims Heal the Wounds?

When the Boston archdiocese agreed to pay $85 million to sexual abuse victims in late 2003, many Church leaders expressed the hope that this gesture would help heal recent wounds and allow both the victims and the Church to move on. "This is an important agreement," said Bishop Wilton D. Gregory, president of the U.S. Conference of Catholic Bishops (as quoted in a September 10, 2003, article in the *Boston Globe*). In Gregory's view, the Boston court cases involving abusive priests were among those that had "precipitated 20 months of soul-searching by the church." He added that the big financial awards to the victims demonstrate "that the church is committed to working out just settlements which seek to meet, to the extent possible, the needs of people who have suffered terribly. We are visibly seeking to heal our wounds caused by sexual abuse and moving forward as promised."

dioceses and parishes across the United States and around the world had already been plagued by increasing financial problems. One cause cited was a small but ongoing drop in church attendance, which in turn contributed to reduced weekly collections. Rising insurance costs have also been cited, as have the high costs of maintaining church buildings, especially older ones needing significant repairs.

The result of these financial setbacks has been an increase in church closings. In May 2004, for instance, the Boston archdiocese announced that it would be forced to close 60, or about one-sixth, of its 357 parishes. Parishioners of some of the affected churches have staged sit-ins in an effort to save their parishes.

Change—Major or Modest?

These and other major issues that concern and divide modern Catholics have increasingly inspired Catholic laypersons to speak out and become more active in Church affairs than they had been in the past. Typically, their approach has not been to denounce or leave the Church. Most remain committed to their basic Catholic beliefs and Catholicism's rich spiritual and cultural heritage. Instead, they say that the Church must, as it

has in the past, reassess and reform itself to meet changing times. In particular, the reformers call for a greater role for the laity in deciding Church policy. As one of the more outspoken members of this group, Carroll recently raised many eyebrows when he said:

> Catholics can never regard priests and bishops uncritically again. . . . The next time that someone announces that the Church is not a democracy, the reply should be that that is precisely the problem. Checks and balances, due process, open procedures, elections, a fully educated community . . . all of this must come into the Church.[57]

In contrast, a number of Catholics feel that Carroll and other reformers go too far and demand too much change too fast. According to this view, the traditional structures and rules of the Church create a framework that imposes needed discipline and humility on the faithful. Some of the traditionalists go so far as to decry a number of the Vatican II reforms as too liberal. In fact, a few bishops broke away from the Vatican and formed their own Catholic organizations following Vatican II. (Shortly before his death in 2005, Pope John Paul II initiated efforts

Catholics protest the closing of two Boston Catholic schools in June 2004. Budgetary woes have forced the Church to reduce many services.

to reconcile the Church and these splinter groups.)

However, even the most traditional Catholics decry the sexual abuse scandals and concede that, to avoid such incidents, the clergy must on occasion institute some modest reforms. The burning question for Catholics in the twenty-first century, then, becomes How much change will occur and how fast? In truth, only time, unfolding circumstances, and the reactions of Church leaders to those circumstances will tell. "Whether such change happens," Keeler and Grimbly say, "whether there will be a Vatican III that sets a new course for the Church, may rest on the men chosen to be the Pope over the next 100 years."[58]

Notes

Introduction: Modern Challenges for an Ancient Faith

1. Hans Kung, *The Catholic Church: A Short History.* New York: Modern Library, 2001, p. xx.
2. Keith Ward, *Christianity: A Short Introduction.* Oxford, England: Oneworld, 2000, pp. 1–2.
3. James Carroll, *Toward a New Catholic Church.* Boston: Houghton Mifflin, 2002, pp. 16–17.

Chapter 1: The Church's Ancient Origins and Birth

4. Justo L. Gonzalez, *The Story of Christianity, Vol. 1: The Early Church to the Dawn of the Reformation.* San Francisco: Harper and Row, 1984, p. 14.
5. Quoted in C.K. Barrett, *The New Testament Background: Selected Documents.* San Francisco: Harper and Row, 1989, p. 247.
6. Luke 24:46–47.
7. Gonzalez, *Story of Christianity,* vol. 1, p. 20.
8. Galatians 1:11–16.
9. Kung, *Catholic Church,* p. 19.
10. Ignatius, *Smyrneans,* quoted in Tony Lane, *Exploring Christian Thought.* Nashville, TN: Thomas Nelson, 1984, p. 13.

Chapter 2: The Spiritual Guide for Medieval Europe

11. A.H.M. Jones, *Constantine and the Conversion of Europe.* Toronto: University of Toronto Press, 1979, p. 207.
12. Quoted in Eusebius, *Ecclesiastical History,* trans. Roy J. Deferrari, 2 vols. Washington, DC: Catholic University of America Press, 1955, vol. 1, p. 269.
13. Lane, *Exploring Christian Thought,* p. 9.
14. Gonzalez, *Story of Christianity,* vol. 1, p. 218.
15. Gonzalez, *Story of Christianity,* vol. 1, p. 296.

Chapter 3: Major Threats: The Reformation and Modernism

16. G.R. Elton, ed., *Renaissance and Reformation: 1300–1648.* New York: Macmillan, 1963, p. 147.
17. Helen Keeler and Susan Grimbly, *The Everything*

Catholicism Book. Avon, MA: Adams Media, 2003, p. 48.

18. Quoted in Eugen Weber, ed., *The Western Tradition: From the Ancient World to Louis XIV.* Boston: D.C. Heath, 1965, p. 337.

19. Quoted in Leon Bernard and Theodore B. Hodges, eds., *Readings in European History.* New York: Macmillan, 1958, p. 227.

20. Quoted in Bernard and Hodges, *Readings*, pp. 248–49.

21. Quoted in Weber, *Western Tradition*, p. 352.

22. Kung, *Catholic Church*, pp. 146, 148–49.

23. Psalms 92:1.

24. Kung, *Catholic Church*, p. 154.

Chapter 4: The Church's Stalwart Anchor: The Pope

25. Matthew 16:18–19.

26. Quoted in Lane, *Exploring Christian Thought*, p. 50.

27. Gonzalez, *Story of Christianity*, vol. 1, pp. 274–75.

28. Keeler and Grimbly, *Catholicism Book*, p. 180.

29. Matthew 28:18–20.

Chapter 5: Fundamental Catholic Beliefs and Practices

30. Quoted in Keeler and Grimbly, *Catholicism Book*, p. 64.

31. Ward, *Christianity*, p. 90.

32. Keeler and Grimbly, *Catholicism Book*, pp. 70, 73.

33. Luke 16:19–21.

34. Augustine, *The City of God*, trans. Marcus Dods, in *Works of Augustine.* Chicago: Encyclopaedia Britannica, 1952, p. 618.

35. *Vatican II Sunday Missal.* Boston: Daughters of St. Paul, 2002.

36. Keeler and Grimbly, *Catholicism Book*, p. 93.

37. Mark 16:17–18.

Chapter 6: Reforms Bring the Church into the Modern Era

38. Keeler and Grimbly, *Catholicism Book*, pp. 54–55.

39. Kung, *Catholic Church*, p. 184.

40. Quoted in "Documents of the Vatican II Council." www.vatican.va/archive/hist_councils/ii_vatican_council/index.htm.

41. Quoted in "Documents of the Vatican II Council."

42. Quoted in Glenn Frankel, "Pope Reconciled with Many, but Made Special Effort with Jews," *Washington Post*, April 8, 2005, p. A17.

43. Jerome J. Langford, *Galileo, Science, and the Church.* Ann Arbor: University of Michigan Press, 1992, p. 185.

44. Quoted in *L'Osservatore Romano*, November 4, 1992.
45. Quoted in "Encyclicals of Pius XII." www.vatican.va/holy_father/pius_xii/encyclicals/index.htm.
46. Quoted in *Catechism of the Catholic Church*. New York: Doubleday, 2003, p. 283.
47. Quoted in *La Stampa*, March 3, 1992.

Chapter 7: The Twenty-First Century: New Demands for Reform
48. Kung, *Catholic Church*, p. 199.
49. Carroll, *New Catholic Church*, pp. 1–2.
50. Quoted in Dan Horn, "Denied a Family, He Left Priesthood," *Cincinnati Enquirer*, May 2, 2004.
51. Horn, "Denied a Family, He Left Priesthood."

52. John Wijngaards, "The 'Tradition' of Not Ordaining Women Priests Was Not Part of the Real Tradition of the Church." www.womenpriests.org/traditio/prej_gen.as.
53. Keeler and Grimbly, *Catholicism Book*, p. 265.
54. Carroll, *New Catholic Church*, p. 5.
55. Quoted in Investigative Staff of the *Boston Globe, Betrayal: The Crisis in the Catholic Church*. New York: Little, Brown, 2002, p. 96.
56. Carroll, *New Catholic Church*, p. 9.
57. Carroll, *New Catholic Church*, p. 15.
58. Keeler and Grimbly, *Catholicism Book*, p. 260.

For Further Reading

Books

Peter Connolly, *Living in the Time of Jesus of Nazareth*. Oxford, England: Oxford University Press, 1983. An easy-to-read introduction to the subject, with beautiful illustrations by the author, the foremost modern illustrator of the ancient world.

Michael Keane, *What You Will See Inside a Catholic Church*. Woodstock, VT: Skylight Paths, 2002. A beautifully illustrated book that takes the reader on a tour of the inside of a typical Catholic church and also explains basic Catholic beliefs.

Michael Keene, *Believers in One God: Judaism, Christianity, Islam*. New York: Cambridge University Press, 1997. An informative summary of the three main monotheistic faiths, written for young readers.

Don Nardo, *Life on a Medieval Pilgrimage*. San Diego: Lucent, 1996. An informative description of the beliefs and customs of devout Christians in medieval Europe.

————, *The Trial of Galileo*. San Diego: Lucent, 2004. Chronicles the famous confrontation between the astronomer Galileo and the Catholic Church, which punished him for arguing that Earth is not the center of all things.

Mary E. Williams, ed., *The Catholic Church*. San Diego: Greenhaven, 2005. A comprehensive examination of several important issues and controversies relating to modern Catholicism.

Web Sites

Ignatius of Antioch (http://en.wiki pedia.org/wiki/Ignatius_of_Anti och). An excellent biography of the important early Church leader who coined the term *Catholic Church*.

In the Footsteps of Paul (www. pbs.org/empires/peterandpaul/fo otsteps). PBS put together this excellent exploration of Paul's ideas, deeds, and the world he lived in. Highly recommended.

John Paul II (www.vatican.va/ holy_father/john_paul_ii). This is the official Vatican biography of one of the most famous and most loved modern popes. Contains numerous links to informative articles about him and the Church.

Reformation Europe (www.ford ham.edu/halsall/mod/modsbook 02.html). A large collection of links to articles about the Reformation and how it changed the Catholic Church, as well as Europe.

Works Consulted

Major Works

Denise L. Carmody and John T. Carmody, *Christianity: An Introduction.* Belmont, CA: Wadsworth, 1995. One of the best short overviews of the evolution of Christian beliefs and rituals and the Church's involvement in social and political issues.

James Carroll, *Toward a New Catholic Church.* Boston: Houghton Mifflin, 2002. A frank examination of modern Catholic issues, controversies, and scandals, supplemented by the author's proposals for various Church reforms.

Henry Chadwick, *The Early Church.* Baltimore: Penguin, 1974. A scholarly but useful discussion of the development of the early Church by an acknowledged authority in the field.

Owen Chadwick, *A History of Christianity.* New York: St. Martin's, 1995. A fine synopsis of Christian events, figures, and cultural influences through the ages.

Everett Ferguson, *Backgrounds for Early Christianity.* Grand Rapids, MI: William B. Eerdmans, 1993. The political, religious, and literary ideas of the Jews, Greeks, and Romans, which provided the base on which Christian thought grew, are explored in detail here.

W.H.C. Frend, *The Rise of Christianity.* Philadelphia: Fortress, 1986. A huge, detailed, and somewhat scholarly look at the subject; this is a classic in the genre.

Justo L. Gonzalez, *The Story of Christianity. Vol. 1: The Early Church to the Dawn of the Reformation.* San Francisco: Harper and Row, 1984. Clearly written, well organized, and thorough, this is one of the better overviews of the events, figures, and intellectual development of early Christianity.

———, *The Story of Christianity. Vol. 2: Reformation to the Present Day.* San Francisco: Harper and Row, 1985. Gonzalez continues his informative chronicle of Christian history, ending his discussion roughly midpoint in the reign of Pope John Paul II.

Hans Kung, *The Catholic Church: A Short History.* New York: Modern Library, 2001. Kung, a controversial priest and excellent historian, provides an accurate overview of Catholic history, doctrine, and issues, while injecting his personal criticisms of various events and leaders.

John McManners, ed., *The Oxford History of Christianity*. Oxford, England: Oxford University Press, 1990. A large compilation of articles by leading scholars about various aspects of Christian history, ideas, and issues.

Jaroslav Pelikan, *The Christian Tradition*. 5 vols. Chicago: University of Chicago Press, 1971. A massive examination of Christian ideas and beliefs through the ages.

E.P. Sanders, *The Historical Figure of Jesus*. New York: Penguin, 1993. An excellent study of what scholars know and do not know about Jesus's actual life, by one of the leading experts in the field.

A.N. Wilson, *Paul: The Mind of the Apostle*. New York: W.W. Norton, 1997. A gripping telling of Paul's story, emphasizing throughout that without his ideas and efforts, Christianity/ Catholicism would likely not have separated from Judaism or become a major faith.

Other Important Works
Primary Sources

Thomas Aquinas, *Summa Theologica*. Trans. Fathers of English Dominican Province. New York: Benziger, 1911.

Augustine, *The City of God*, trans. Marcus Dods, in *Works of Augustine*. Chicago: Encyclopaedia Britannica, 1952.

C.K. Barrett, *The New Testament Background: Selected Documents*. San Francisco: Harper and Row, 1989.

Leon Bernard and Theodore B. Hodges, eds., *Readings in European History*. New York: Macmillan, 1958.

Henry Bettenson and Chris Maunder, eds., *Documents of the Christian Church*. London: Oxford University Press, 1999.

Catechism of the Catholic Church. New York: Doubleday, 2003.

"Documents of the Vatican II Council." www.vatican.va/archive/hist_councils/ii_vatican_council/index.htm.

G.R. Elton, ed., *Renaissance and Reformation: 1300–1648*. New York: Macmillan, 1963.

"Encyclicals of Pius XII." www.vatican.va/holy_father/pius_xii/encyclicals/index.htm.

Eusebius, *Ecclesiastical History*. Trans. Roy J. Deferrari. 2 vols. Washington, DC: Catholic University of America Press, 1955.

Josephus, *The Jewish Antiquities*. Trans. L.H. Feldman. Cambridge, MA: Harvard University Press, 1967.

Howard C. Kee, ed., *The Origins of Christianity: Sources and Documents.* Englewood Cliffs, NJ: Prentice-Hall, 1973.

Tony Lane, *Exploring Christian Thought.* Nashville, TN: Thomas Nelson, 1984.

Naphtali Lewis and Meyer Reinhold, eds., *Roman Civilization, Sourcebook 2: The Empire.* New York: Harper and Row, 1966.

J.H. Robinson, ed., *Readings on European History.* New York: Ginn, 1904.

Brian Tierney, ed., *The Middle Ages. Vol. 1: Sources of Medieval History.* New York: Knopf, 1973.

Eugen Weber, ed., *The Western Tradition: From the Ancient World to Louis XIV.* Boston: D.C. Heath, 1965.

Modern Sources

Denise S. Amos and Dan Horn, "Priests, Nuns, Vanishing from Classroom," *Cincinnati Enquirer,* May 4, 2004.

John D. Crossan, *The Historical Jesus: The Life of a Mediterranean Jewish Peasant.* San Francisco: HarperCollins, 1992.

Eric R. Dodds, *Pagan and Christian in an Age of Anxiety.* New York: Cambridge University Press, 1991.

Glenn Frankel, "Pope Reconciled with Many, but Made Special Effort with Jews," *Washington Post.* April 8, 2005.

Charles Freeman, *Egypt, Greece, and Rome.* New York: Oxford University Press, 2004.

Michael Grant, *Constantine the Great: The Man and His Times.* New York: Scribner's, 1994.

———, *Jesus: An Historian's View of the Gospels.* New York: Scribner's, 1977.

———, *The Jews in the Roman World.* London: Weidenfeld and Nicolson, 1973.

Roberta L. Harris, *The World of the Bible.* New York: Thames and Hudson, 1995.

Dan Horn, "Denied a Family, He Left Priesthood," *Cincinnati Enquirer,* May 2, 2004.

Investigative Staff of the *Boston Globe, Betrayal: The Crisis in the Catholic Church.* New York: Little, Brown, 2002.

A.H.M. Jones, *Constantine and the Conversion of Europe.* Toronto: University of Toronto Press, 1979.

Helen Keeler and Susan Grimbly, *The Everything Catholicism Book.* Avon, MA: Adams Media, 2003.

Hans Kung, *Reforming the Church Today.* Edinburgh, Scotland: T. and T. Clark, 1992.

Jerome J. Langford, *Galileo, Science, and the Church.* Ann Arbor: University of Michigan Press, 1992.

Ramsay MacMullen, *Christianizing the Roman Empire, A.D. 100–400.* New Haven, CT: Yale University Press, 1984.

Michael Paulson, "Terms Leave Archdiocese Facing New Strains," *Boston Globe,* September 10, 2003.

Howard F. Vos, *Introduction to Church History.* Nashville, TN: Thomas Nelson and Sons, 1994.

J.W.C. Wand, *A History of the Early Church to A.D. 500.* London: Methuen, 1965.

Keith Ward, *Christianity: A Short Introduction.* Oxford, England: Oneworld, 2000.

John Wijngaards, "The 'Tradition' of Not Ordaining Women Priests Was Not Part of the Real Tradition of the Church." www. women priests.org/traditio/prej_gen.asp.

Garry Wills, *Papal Sin: Structures of Deceit.* New York: Doubleday, 2000.

A.N. Wilson, *Jesus.* London: Sinclair-Stevenson, 1992.

Index

Picture Credits

About the Author

In addition to his acclaimed volumes on ancient civilizations, historian Don Nardo has published several books about Christian origins and key historic court trials run by Church officials, including *The Rise of Christianity, The Trial of Joan of Arc*, and *The Trial of Galileo*. Mr. Nardo also writes screenplays and teleplays and composes music. He lives with his wife, Christine, in Massachusetts.